SUCCESSFUL
AUTHOR FAQS

DISCOVER THE ART OF WRITING, THE BUSINESS OF
PUBLISHING, AND THE JOY OF WIELDING WORDS

PETER LYLE DEHAAN

ISBN:
979-8-88809-050-3 (e-book)
979-8-88809-051-0 (paperback)
979-8-88809-052-7 (hardcover)
979-8-88809-053-4 (audiobook)

Library of Congress Control Number: 2023911976

Published by Rock Rooster Books, Grand Rapids, Michigan

Credits:
Editorial consultant: Claudia Volkman
Copy editor: Robyn Mulder
Proofreader: Julie Harbison
Cover design: Cassidy Wierks
Author photo: Jordan Leigh Photography

DEDICATION

To my fellow writers. May you enjoy success and find fulfillment on your author journey.

CONTENTS

BEHIND THESE FAQS

Peter Lyle DeHaan makes a full-time living through his writing.

In 1982 he sold his first piece for an astounding $300 and never looked back. Since then, he has written hundreds of articles, thousands of blog posts, and scores of books, with over one hundred ideas in queue.

Since 2001 he has been president and editor-in-chief of his own publishing company, producing magazines, e-publications, websites and now publishing his own books. And since 2015 he's worked as a commercial freelance writer, earning a nice five-figure income from it.

This lifetime of experience gives Peter a vast amount of knowledge to pull from, and for those situations he hasn't personally encountered, he draws insights from the many writing and publishing podcasts he listens to each week.

This book covers the frequently asked questions writers have posed to him over the years as a publisher, editor, freelancer, and author, as well as a writing conference speaker, critique group leader, and writing and publishing blogger.

1. The Intentional Writer

If writing matters to you—and it must, since you're reading this book—let's start with some basic big-picture ideas to point us in the right direction and help us move forward.

Whether you're just beginning or have pursued writing for a while, these items apply to every writer.

Is It Worth It?

Question: *I want to write, but the more I learn about this as a career or even a side pursuit, the more overcome I feel. Is writing worth it?*

Answer: Most definitely!

First, if writing were easy, everyone would do it. Though anyone who knows how to read can also write, few people can write well. That's what being a writer is: exercising our ability to string words together with excellence.

As with any worthwhile endeavor, it takes time to develop skill as a writer. As writers, we're always learning and always growing. Each piece we write has the potential to be better than the piece before it. And each year our ability can surpass last year. Writing is a journey of discovery that lasts a lifetime.

Second, if you have a passion to write, then pursue it with full-out abandon. Don't dismiss writing for a more profitable pursuit. If you do, you'll always regret it. But that doesn't mean being a full-time writer. Most authors write and do something else. They may have a full-time job and write on the side. Or they may focus on writing but have a "side hustle" or two to help pay the bills.

Writing is art, and it is science. Embrace both. Pursue both. Merge both to produce words that sing or words that sell. What joy we realize as we learn to write like that.

Third, writing is a smart way to avoid job obsolescence. In the ever-evolving labor market—which changes faster every year—the career most people start with is seldom the career they end with. Writing, along with a few other skills, sidesteps the threat of obsolescence. Yes, the form of our publication will change—it already has and will continue to do so—but the skill to arrange the underlying words will persist.

People who have mastered the art of writing will always have something to do—even if we can't now imagine what that might look like.

Fourth, writing embraces a new way to earn a living. As forty-hour-a-week jobs become less available and less desirable, twenty-first-century workers piece together a variety of pursuits to produce income, achieve better work-life balance, and find vocational fulfillment.

This approach includes freelancing, contract work, and subcontracting, with many writers leading the charge in these areas. With this mindset to guide us, today's writers can forge ahead to produce a life with variety, purpose, and fulfillment. And you can join them in this quest.

How amazing is that?

Yes, without a doubt, pursuing a career in writing is worth the effort.

Takeaway: When discouraged, remember the joy of writing, and hold on to your dream to be an author.

Finding Balance

Question: How can I balance writing, work, and life?

Answer: In my pursuit of work-life balance, it seems something is always slipping, with writing, work, and life residing in constant tension. Yes, at times I may go a couple of days keeping everything in balance, but one little bump and the whole illusion falls apart.

We should always consider this issue of work-life balance and make whatever tweaks we can to move closer to achieving a sustainable existence.

Each writer needs to figure out this dilemma, to learn what works best for themselves and their situation. Something common to all writers is that the solution requires intentionality and self-discipline.

One fact we can know for sure is if we don't strive to make balance happen, we'll never come close.

Takeaway: You may never find sustainable work-life balance, but you can find a solution that works for you and your situation.

FINDING TIME TO WRITE

Question: *How do you find time to write?*

Answer: Most writers face this dilemma at one point or another. The problem, however, dwells in the question. We don't need to find time to write as much as we need to make time.

We each have twenty-four hours in our day. While work and sleep occupy part of each day, we exercise some degree of control over the rest. We decide what we will do with it. We can choose to write or opt to do something else.

Before you say, "But my situation is different," let me agree. Everyone's situation is different.

Then let me ask how much time you spend each week watching TV or going on social media. Time spent on these activities presents a prime opportunity to write instead.

If writing is important to us, we'll make time to write. We may write a little or a lot. We may write every day or only once a week, but we must make it happen.

If you can carve out one hour a week, every week, and write 500 words, by the end of the year you will have written 26,000 words.

If you can carve out ten minutes a day, every day, and write one hundred words each time, by the end of the year you'll have written 36,500 words.

The key is to form a plan that works for your schedule and then follow it.

Takeaway: Don't *find* time to write, *make* time.

QUANTITY VERSUS QUALITY

Question: *What's one thing you wished you had done differently in your writing career?*

Answer: For years I worked to write faster, but I made no effort to write better. Though I did improve, my progress proceeded at the pace of a snail.

Yes, the experience of writing so much produced results, but I didn't realize the maximum benefit from it because I hadn't studied the craft.

When I got serious about improving as a writer, I had to force myself to write slower, with more deliberation. Now, after many years of focusing on the craft, my speed has returned and then advanced.

But I lost a couple of decades focusing on quantity instead of quality. If I could have a do-over, I'd address content first and not worry about speed.

Takeaway: Always strive to improve as a writer.

DICTATION

Question: I've heard of writers who claim to write fast using dictation, what are your thoughts on it?

Answer: I'm a huge fan of dictation and use it for all my writing, not only my first draft, but even as I edit. Using dictation, I can approach about two thousand words an hour, compared to about one thousand words typing. My dictated words come out in pretty good shape, about 90 percent of the way there.

Although some people claim five thousand words an hour from dictation, I'm not one of them. Yes, I talk fast and could dictate ten thousand words per hour, but those words would require so much editing as to make them worthless. Therefore, I slow down, think about what I want to say, and say it. I'm pleased with the results and the speed.

I pursued dictation for two reasons. One was to write faster. The other was to protect my aching wrists. Despite doing the recommended exercises and taking frequent breaks, my wrists often throbbed after writing several hours a day, day after day.

Thanks to dictation, my wrists don't hurt anymore, but now I need to protect my voice. Drink lots of water when dictating. Avoid carbonated beverages, milk, and coffee.

By the way, I'm a poor candidate for dictation. First, you should dictate in complete sentences, but I don't. Most of the time, I don't know how a sentence will end when I frame the beginning in my mind. Therefore, my dictation gushes out as a disjointed hodgepodge of sentence fragments and phrases.

Second, I don't enunciate well. And I often pronounce the same word two ways. This trait makes it hard for the dictation software and requires a critical eye to catch errors, which are sometimes comical, albeit infuriating.

As a result, my dictated work needs a bit more editing. Though my overall production speed using dictation isn't two times faster, it certainly produces a more than 50 percent improvement.

For full disclosure, using dictation has had unexpected side effects. It has resulted in a slowdown of my typing speed and has been a further hit to my spelling challenges. Still, dictation stands as a more-than-equitable trade-off, increasing my production speed, while avoiding carpal tunnel surgery.

Takeaway: Though dictation isn't for everyone, it's worth trying.

Don't Forget to Back Up Your Files

Question: I know I should back up my writing, but I don't. What do you recommend?

Answer: Backing up our files is essential. This issue isn't a matter of *if* we lose some of our writing but of *when*. Having a good backup is essential.

I learned this lesson the hard way early on in my career. As a tech writer, I lost a week's worth of work because I went home one Friday without backing up my writing for the week. A power spike left the only file of my recent work unreadable.

Each time I finish a writing session, I make a copy of the document on my computer and another on a second computer, both of which upload to different remote backup providers. I also make a copy of all my files each week and save them on an external hard drive.

For a simple backup option, sign up for a web-based email account and send yourself a copy of your work each time you finish writing.

There are also many providers that provide offsite file storage. Some offer a free basic plan, but this may require some effort on your part.

Other providers automatically back up files to the cloud. The monthly cost of a basic plan is about the price of a premium cup of coffee. When you consider the time we invest in writing, this backup step provides inexpensive insurance. This is what I recommend.

Takeaway: Back up your work every time you write.

WRITERS MUST BE READERS

Question: Will reading help me understand what is marketable before I spend hours writing something that's not?

Answer: Reading helps give us clarity on what to write, how to write (and not write), and what is marketable.

Read in your genre (for fiction writers) or subject area (for nonfiction writers). Make that your focus, but also read outside of them as well. Good writing is good writing regardless of genre or topic. And poor writing is also poor writing. Learn from both.

As we read, we'll see styles, techniques, and writing voices that delight us, while other ones will irritate us. Never copy another author whose writing you admire, but do learn from them. Take what you like and adapt it. Also discover what you don't like and avoid it.

In addition to reading widely, talk to others in the industry, especially agents, editors, and publishers. They can provide a lot of valuable information, including insight into what is marketable.

But focus on reading. Read regularly, read widely, and read a lot. You will be a better writer because of it.

Takeaway: Reading helps make us better writers.

FIND TIME TO READ

Question: You say writers need to read, but how do you find the time?

Answer: Finding time to read is a constant struggle. As with making time to write, we need to make time to read.

For me the decision often comes down to watching TV or reading. Sometimes TV wins and other times reading wins. Often, the choice I make hinges on how good the book is versus how much a show or movie calls me.

I strive to keep my TV watch list short and my book list interesting. I also give myself the freedom to stop reading any book that bores me or turns me off. If I didn't allow myself this option, TV would grab my attention most of the time.

The point is, we all have some degree of discretionary time, whether it's TV, movies, social media, going out, leisure activities, or even a nap. We can choose to do these alternate pursuits or to read. For me, I've cut back on TV to read more—and I'm glad I did.

Some writers, however, including myself, feel that watching TV and, even more so, movies help us learn about plot, character development, and good (or bad) storytelling.

Takeaway: Scale back on entertainment and social media to read more.

Determining Your Reading List

Question: You say it's important for writers to read. What do you select for your reading list?

Answer: Carving out time to read and still have time to write, while also attending to the rest of life challenges me. Yet I know it's critical to invest in reading to better inform my writing.

Some people, folks more disciplined than I, chart a reading course for the year. They make strategic picks of fiction books from different genres, both current and classic, along with memoir and nonfiction. By the end of the year, they've sampled a broad array of literature.

In an ideal situation, I'd do the same. But I don't. To find the motivation to read, I must select books that grab my attention. If the book bores me, I'll lay it down and stop.

Here's what works for me.

First, I prefer novels. I select popular (or once popular) books, books made into movies (since I enjoy movies), books friends recommend, books from favorite authors, and books by friends. I stir in an occasional nonfiction book because it's good for me.

Though I read in spurts, I complete twenty to forty books a year.

My approach isn't ideal, but it's better than not reading at all.

Takeaway: Be strategic in what you read, but always keep it enjoyable.

Reading Goals for Writers

Question: I get that it's important for writers to read. What are your goals when reading books?

Answer: Because I need to push myself to read, my overarching requirement is that the book must interest me. This approach limits the range of what I read. Some people insist on reading the classics, even if boring. I don't.

So my first goal is to read what entertains me, or sometimes, what educates me. Have you ever put a book down and never picked it up again? I have. I never want to write a book like that. Seeing this lack of interest happen in other books helps me avoid it in mine.

My second goal is to identify what I like in the books I read, so I can apply it to my own work. And what I don't like, so I can avoid it.

Here are some other characteristics I look for as I read:

- What keeps me turning pages?

- What tempts me to skim?

- What causes me to stop reading altogether?

- What confuses me? How would I edit the passage to make it clearer?

- What delights me?

- What bores me?

- When I get to the end of a chapter, am I content to lay the book down or do I want to turn the page?

- Do the words, sentences, paragraphs, and chapters flow with ease?

- What speed bumps take me out of the reading?

And here are some specific nonfiction items:

- Is the book well-organized?

- Are the chapters laid out logically?

- Does the book contain "filler" content that only adds to the page count but not the book's value?

And these questions apply to fiction:

- How does the author layer in foreshadowing?

- How does the author write and format dialogue?

- Does the writing pull me into the story?

Regardless of what I'm reading, I listen to my editor's internal commentary. Since I do a lot of editing as a periodical publisher, I can't just turn off my editor brain when I read—even though I try.

What I learn from reading informs my own writing.

Takeaway: When you read, read with purpose.

INVEST IN YOUR WRITING

Question: What's the second biggest mistake you've made in your writing career?

Answer: A key mistake I made early in my career was not investing in learning the craft of writing. Though I put in the time, for years I didn't invest money. But taking the cheap way out slowed my progress.

Here are some investments I now make to become a better writer:

- Study magazines about writing and publishing.

- Read books and blogs about writing and publishing.

- Listen to podcasts about writing and publishing.

- Attend writing conferences.

- Hire developmental editors, copy editors, and proofreaders.

- Join online classes about specific writing-related topics.

- Take part in online writing communities.

- Hire mentors and teachers.

Of course, none of these learning opportunities would help if I wasn't applying them every day by writing. This list is long, but don't let it overwhelm you. Pick one item to invest in and add more over time.

Also, not everything on this list costs money. In some cases, our only cost is time. Reading blogs and listening to podcasts are cost-free ways to learn about writing and publishing.

Takeaway: Invest in your writing now to produce a return later.

10,000 Hours

Question: What's the 10,000-Hour Rule? Does it apply to writers?

Answer: Malcolm Gladwell, in his 2008 book Outliers, explains the 10,000-Hour Rule. That's how many hours it takes to master something. It applies to writing just as much as any other skill. Keep in mind, this number isn't the amount of time it takes to start writing. Ten thousand hours is how much time it takes to do it well.

In similar fashion, others talk about needing to write one million words. I can't find the original source for this stat, but I agree with the principle. Though it might not be a million words, it's a lot. I don't know my lifetime word count, but I estimated it a few years ago. I had surpassed one million words when I began to find my voice and enjoy a comfortable rhythm of writing. As far as number of hours, I have no idea, but it exceeds ten thousand.

Before you panic, let's put this generality into perspective.

The first thousand words I wrote as an adult was an article that I sold for an impressive paycheck. And the second thousand words I wrote resulted in another published article, though it was for the byline and not the money.

In fact, most of the first fifty thousand words I wrote enjoyed publication in various trade publications. Though I didn't earn a penny from any of them, I learned invaluable lessons. This work taught me how to meet deadlines, write when I didn't feel like it, and discover what worked and what didn't. In doing so, I built a following, received feedback, and earned several "writer of the year" awards.

To be fair, I also wrote some books early in my career. They sit in obscurity on my hard drive and will take a fair amount of work to get them to where they need to be. I doubt it's worth the effort.

Don't let ten thousand hours or one million words discourage you. You may enjoy initial success much sooner than that. But view writing as a journey. Investing ten thousand hours and writing one million words is part of that journey.

Takeaway: It takes time to write well, but that doesn't rule out enjoying some early wins.

2. CRAFT

As writers, it's critical to always strive to improve what we do. There are scores of great craft books to help us improve our writing, but here are some questions from beginning and intermediate writers.

Tips to Improve as a Writer

Question: *What do you do to improve as a writer?*

Answer: Here are the actions I pursue to improve as a writer:

- Write regularly.

- Read a lot (I struggle the most with this tip).

- Study writing.

- Listen to writing and publishing podcasts.

- Follow writing blogs.

- Participate in writers' groups.

- Attend writing conferences.

- But the most important tip is to write.

These tips helped my writing improve. May they do the same for you.

Takeaway: To be a writer, you must write.

WRITE EVERY DAY

Question: *What's the number one thing you did to become a better writer?*

Answer: The single most important step I ever took as a writer was to commit to write every day.

This principle to write every day is shorthand for "write regularly." At first I wrote five days a week, Monday through Friday. Then I made it six days and later, seven. Now I've cut back to five. This is because managing dozens of published books takes time.

This rhythm works for me in this season of my life.

Through all these variations, the one constant is that on every writing day I get up and write. Whether I feel like it or not, I sit down and write. I commit to at least an hour each day, but my goal is to write much more. On most days, I do.

Until I began writing regularly, it was ancillary. Now it's central. My focus on writing every day has made all the difference.

Takeaway: Write regularly, even when you don't feel like it.

Work Up to Writing a Book

Question: I want to write a novel. How should I go about this?

Answer: Before writing a book, start with short stories (for fiction writers) or articles (for nonfiction writers). Most of the elements required for short pieces carry over to longer works.

Writing short pieces lets us experiment. We can have fast successes and failures. I'd rather experiment with a new technique on a 1,000-word piece of flash fiction or article than commit to an 80,000-word book only to find out it wasn't working once I finished writing.

Here are some other benefits of starting short:

- Article and short story experience will help us edit and polish our longer works more effectively before sending them off to a professional editor.

- We can use our articles and short stories as a lead magnet to build our mailing list and share with fans between books. And for fiction, this tip is even more compelling if the short stories are about our novel's characters.

- We can submit a short work to an anthology, which will give us a writing credit prior to publishing our book.

- A nonfiction book's chapters can resemble an article (or blog post). There's a thesis statement or hook, the argument or body of the text, and a strong conclusion or memorable wrap up.

- Similarly, a novel's chapters are often like short stories, with a beginning hook, page-turning middle, and satisfying end or can't-put-it-down cliffhanger. Short story experience will help us determine chapter breaks, as well as starting chapters with more punch and ending with more flair.

- Also, short stories about characters in our novel will help us understand their backstory. Then we can write, rewrite, and edit them more convincingly.

Once you're comfortable with short, then you can increase the length of what you write. For both fiction and nonfiction, the goal is to start short and then go long.

With many short pieces to your credit, you're more ready to write a book. Whether you're a planner (plotter) or discovery writer (a pantser—you write by the seat of your pants), you should have some idea of where your book is going before you start writing.

For nonfiction I know my theme, working title, and arc. And I have enough of an outline to guide my writing. For novels I begin with a list of characters and basic bios, a story arc, the plot, key elements, and a chapter outline. If I'm writing tens of thousands of words, I don't want to waste effort.

For some writers this prep work stifles their creativity, but it motivates me. Pick the method that works for you and start writing.

Many fiction writers admit to completing several novels before one is good enough to publish. Perhaps they didn't first hone their craft with short pieces. So don't expect your first effort to succeed. If it does, that's great. But be prepared to crank out a couple of books before you produce one that's good enough to publish.

Takeaway: Start with writing short pieces and work up to books.

Changing Writing Conventions

Question: *I recently learned to not end a sentence with two spaces. I want to stay current with other changes in writing conventions. Is there a site, a book, an app, or a publication I can purchase?*

Answer: Writing conventions continually change, but there is no one-stop resource—such as a website, book, app, or magazine—that tracks and compiles these changes. And even if there were, writers would argue over the recommendations, anyway.

Instead, we need to figure this out for ourselves. Here's how I work to keep up with ever-changing writing trends:

- Participate in critique groups.

- Network with other writers.

- Go to writing conferences.

- Take advantage of every opportunity to have a professional editor look at my work.

- Learn from the recommendations of editors.

- Study the latest edition of the Chicago Manual of Style.

- Look at the conventions followed in recent books produced by major publishers, while noting that they, too, make mistakes.

The main point is to not write in isolation.

Takeaway: Stay current on ever-changing writing expectations.

WRITING VOICE AND STYLE

Question: *Are voice and style the same?*

Answer: Though sometimes used interchangeably, *voice* and *style* have differences. On a basic level, think of your writing voice as personality and your writing style as technique. Voice may be a subset of the larger category of style. There is overlap.

Voice comprises our content, perspective, and temperament. It includes our word choice, rhythm, and tone. A writer's voice allows us to identify the author behind the writing.

For instance, my writing voice (I hope) is conversational and easy to follow. It's neither formal nor informal, but it veers toward informal. I aim for clarity over cleverness. I take prideful pleasure in alliteration. And I relish using trios of words, phrases, or ideas.

Of course, this description blurs into writing style. See why some people use the words interchangeably?

My writing style uses complete sentences and avoids semicolons. I vary sentence length. And I often start sentences with conjunctions and have no qualms about ending with prepositions. I follow standard formatting and punctuation, deviating from them only to make a point, but never to appear cool or exhibit snark. I aim to write at the sixth-grade level. (This book clocks in at 6.9 on the Flesch-Kincaid Grade Level scale.)

As you continue to write, your writing voice will emerge, and your writing style will solidify.

Takeaway: You are unique, and your writing should reflect that.

IDENTIFYING SPEAKERS IN DIALOGUE

Question: *What is the best way to identify speakers in dialogue?*

Answer: How to identify speakers in dialogue lies with your writing voice and style. Note that memoirists and even nonfiction writers should know how to write good dialogue.

Here are some ideas to consider:

Use Colorful Tags: Tag your dialogue with any descriptive word other than said, such as exclaimed, interjected, sputtered, yelled, and so forth. I learned this advice in middle school and followed it for many years.

Now the recommendation is to avoid this suggestion, as it signals lazy writing, though this view could change in the future.

I prefer to show the speaker's emotion instead of stating it. For example: Bruce narrowed his gaze and pursed his lips. "I can't believe you did that," he said.

I far prefer that to "I can't believe you did that," Bruce snarled.

I use a descriptive tag only if I feel it will make the passage stronger or add clarity.

Only Use Said: While we need to identify the speaker, some people feel the use of anything other than said is an annoying speed bump. Others even recommend using said for questions, as in: "How long will you be gone?" Gene said.

I use said most of the time when I need a dialogue tag, but I still use asked for questions.

Avoid Tags: My preference, however, is to use context to identify the speaker. In this way I minimize the use of dialogue tags and let the surrounding text show who the reader is, as in this exchange:

Ben stared at the first-edition book in his trembling hands. "You mean I get to keep this?"

Sue's eyes danced. "Yes, it's a gift."

"I don't know what to say."

"How about 'Thank you'?"

"I so appreciate this." Ben blinked three times, fighting to hold back tears. "Thank you. This is so wonderful."

This passage contains no dialogue tags, but the context shows Ben as the first speaker and Sue, the second. Since this dialogue is a rapid exchange, readers understand that Ben replies to Sue, and she responds in the fourth line. Then to make sure readers don't get lost, the fifth line confirms Ben is talking.

This approach takes more work to write, but it seems this method is the current trend and strikes me as powerful writing. But don't feel bound to follow this technique for every piece of dialogue. It will be tedious to write—and to read.

Though I now lean toward this final approach to dialogue, I also use the other two when it helps to produce a clear and interesting passage.

Takeaway: Mastering dialogue is essential for fiction, which benefits memoir and even nonfiction writers.

Points of View

Question: *What are perspectives in writing and which should I use?*

Answer: There are many books written on this subject.

Most people use the terms *perspective* and *point of view* interchangeably—which is what I learned in High School English—but others make a distinction between them, claiming that *point of view* is the correct term for this discussion.

Here is a basic overview:

First Person Point of View: First person point of view uses *I*, as in *I said . . .* or *I went . . .*

For example: I went to the bookstore to buy the latest book by my favorite author.

Second Person Point of View: Second person point of view uses *you*, as in *You said . . .* or *You went . . .*

For example: You went to the store to buy a journal and pen.

In fiction, second person is hard to write (and to read), so most authors avoid it. As an exercise, I wrote a piece of flash fiction in second person, present tense. It was tedious.

Sometimes nonfiction writers use second person for *how-to* and *self-help* pieces. But second person can come across as pedantic or talking down to readers. Use it with care.

Third Person Point of View: Third person point of view uses *he, she,* and *they*, as in *He said . . .* or *They went . . .*

For example: They went to a book signing to see the famous author.

Two Types of Third Person Point of View: There are two flavors of third person: *Limited*, where the reader knows only what the point of view character can observe or think and *Omniscient,* where the narrator knows what everyone thinks.

Third person omniscient is out of favor and seldom recommended anymore—though many of the classics, including much of the Bible, use third person omniscient.

Writing Tense: For each of these four considerations we have two additional options: *present tense* (what is happening now) and *past tense* (what has already happened).

Past tense is easier to use, and first person is more natural for most writers. When we tell stories about ourselves to our friends, we use first person, past tense.

Therefore, in your writing, you might want to start with first person, past tense, as in "I wondered which point of view I should use for my book." Then if you want, move to third person, past tense, as in "Sue wondered which point of view to use for her short story."

Note that some genres have specific expectations for point of view and tense, which you should follow.

Takeaway: Know the different points of view, but use the one you feel most comfortable with.

THIRD PERSON OMNISCIENT

Question: Why is third person omniscient out of favor?

Answer: Though we could attribute it to a trend, the best explanation I have is that we're conditioned to watching TV and movies, which limit us to the camera's vantage (third person limited, if you will). As readers we expect books to follow this convention.

When I began writing, I preferred third person omniscient because third person limited seemed, well, too limiting. Third person omniscient was also easier to write because it didn't restrict me to one point of view per scene.

But those days are gone. Few books published today use third person omniscient point of view. Though this trend could reverse itself, I don't see it happening anytime soon.

Takeaway: Avoid writing in third person omniscient.

How to Format Numbers

Question: In your writing, I notice you refer to one and two with words, but with 150 you use numbers instead. Which is right?

Answer: Properly formatting numbers is an interesting quandary, and I wish there was one answer. There are two main rules that apply:

1. Write out single-digit numbers (one through nine) and use digits for the numbers 10 and higher, or

2. Write out one hundred and everything less. Use numbers for everything greater than one hundred.

Both these rules apply to whole numbers. If a number has a decimal point, always use digits.

Online writing usually follows rule one, while fiction usually follows rule two. Nonfiction can go either way.

Though the pragmatic part of me wants to follow the first rule—because it lets me write faster—I make myself follow rule two. For the types of writing I do, rule two works best. I even follow rule two for my online work. (Though I'm sure you could find many times I didn't follow this convention. Such is the case when our writing evolves.)

In addition, some style guides say to write out common numbers and use digits for all others. Applying this advice would result in:

- one thousand

- 1,051

- one million

- 999,157

Of course, there are special cases. For example, if a sentence begins with a number, *always* spell it. If this format looks awkward, rewrite the sentence so that it doesn't start with a number.

In this case: "One thousand, two hundred and fifty-seven people were present . . ." becomes "An attendance of 1,257. . ."

Takeaway: Learn how to properly represent numbers in your writing.

Writing and Artificial Intelligence (AI)

Question: *Does using artificial intelligence to help me write make me less of a writer?*

Answer: When most people think about using artificial intelligence to write, their mind goes to people who may abuse the technology. Yes, some people will use AI to churn out sub-par books. But don't worry about them.

Instead, look to how you use AI. View AI as a tool to help you write better, just like word processing software or spell and grammar checkers.

Your goal as a writer should be to produce the best possible book you can to delight your readers, be it to entertain or educate. Use AI tools to help achieve this goal, and don't worry about others who may misuse it.

If you tap AI as a writing tool to enhance your work, you can be satisfied that you're properly using it and not abusing it. Then, with a clear conscience, you can move forward to produce excellent work, which should be the goal of every writer.

Takeaway: Embrace AI as a tool to help you write better, and don't worry about how others may use—or abuse—it.

3. Planning

With great passion, writers debate whether to plan a book or discover it as they write. But the planning (plotting) versus discovery (pantsing: you write by the seat of your pants) deliberation isn't an either/or matter. It exists on a continuum, with all writers doing some of both. The question becomes how much we plan and how much we discover as we write.

For discovery writers, the process is simple. Start with an idea, scene, or premise. Write it. Then decide what follows. Continue this process until you've completed the entire book or piece. For planning, an outline—and its various forms—stands as a key organizational tool to guide writing.

Remember, all writers use some combination of these two processes. Only the ratio changes.

WHICH APPROACH IS BEST?

Question: I understand some people write using an outline, while others discover what comes next as they write. Which is better?

Answer: Writers often wonder and debate about using an outline to guide their writing versus discovering their content as they write. Let me forever end that debate (not really).

Use whatever approach works best for you.

When writing a short story, article, or blog post, I often start with a title, opening line, or concept. Then I start writing to see where it takes me. (Sometimes I have the last line in mind and write to get there.) Though this method may result in extra content to cut, those words often become part of another piece. But recently I've been writing to hit bullet points, which is a basic outline.

Conversely, when I start writing a book—whether fiction or nonfiction—I always have an outline. This guide gives me structure to flow from one item to the next, without wasting time or words. Cutting 20 percent of a 300-word blog post (60 words) isn't a big deal, but cutting 20 percent of a 50,000-word book (10,000 words) is painful.

But even though I use an outline for books, I still discover delightful ideas along the way. When I do, it's an exciting bonus that I'm happy to work into the text. Then I update my outline, which helps me stay organized.

Takeaway: Use the writing approach that works best for you.

Planning a Book

Question: People tell me I need an outline before I start writing. How do I make a writing outline?

Answer: That's an interesting question. Outlining—at least my version of it—is natural for me, so I've never given much thought about how to do it.

In middle school, however, my teachers taught me the "proper" way to do an outline. Their method was rigid, and it had rules. These restrictions caused me to hate outlining. If you had a similar experience, ignore *every* rule you've ever heard about outlining. Outlining is a tool to help you, not a painful exercise to produce angst.

Your outline can take any form you want as long as it accomplishes your objective, which is to guide your writing. For simpler projects, my outline is often a bulleted list. That's enough because that's all I need. For more involved works, my outline has more structure, with main points and subpoints and sometimes even sub-subpoints.

To give a picture of outlining (planning), envision going on a vacation.

Some people get in their car and start driving, without a destination. They discover their vacation as they go. This idea is analogous to discovery writing. But this method isn't the most effective way to be intentional with a vacation.

Instead, you know where you're starting from and know where you're going to. You have some stops you want to make along the way. And the shortest path to your destination may not be the ideal one, so you plan some side trips. Put your starting point, your ending point, and each stop you'll make on your trip in chronological order. This results in your vacation outline.

Now add other information (if you want), such as where you'll stay each night, the cost, and any other expenses you'll incur. You might even note the estimated times for each leg of your journey and each stop—or that might be too much planning for you. The point is to include just enough preparation to make your vacation enjoyable without being constrictive.

You want to follow the same planning approach before you write an article, short story, or book. Your writing outline will begin with your starting point for the piece, your opening hook or setting. It will end with your conclusion or climax. In between, list each point (for nonfiction) or scene (for fiction). This information will help you move from the beginning to the end.

Put your writing outline in whatever form will be most useful to you, and include only the relevant information you need to write effectively. Add details only if they will benefit your writing process. And remember, just because you have an outline doesn't mean you must follow it. As you write, you may discover you want to take a side trip or even head in the opposite direction. That's okay. Your outline is a tool to help you write, not a shackle to limit your creativity.

Now, armed with your outline, go write.

Takeaway: An outline is a plan to guide our writing, nothing more.

Planning a Series

Question: *What is a good method to outline a series?*

Answer: Just as you can outline a book, you can also outline a series.

Consider your series outline as listing the main objective you want to accomplish for each book. Just as each book will have an arc, your series will also have one. Your series outline should reflect the series arc.

Your series outline can be as simple as a bullet point for each book. That's what I start with. Or you can add more substance to it, but I suggest you save additional details for the book outline, which you will need for each book in the series.

Outlining a series is fun, and I recommend it. Knowing a series arc, through its outline, can inform your writing of each book in the series.

For example, if you know your primary character for book three, make a subtle introduction in book one. This restrained reveal will delight your readers when they re-encounter that person two books later. Or if book eight has a plot development you worry may seem a bit contrived, with shrewd finesse lay the groundwork for it in books two, five, and seven. This unexpected development in book eight will still surprise your readers, but they won't feel you forced it because you prepared them for it in earlier books.

Keep in mind that if you're a discovery writer you *can't* insert any delicious titbits into earlier books—unless they're not yet published.

But with a series outline to guide your writing, you can foreshadow what is to come in future books.

In addition, having a series outline will keep you from wasting time writing passages you will later cut. And your plan will help make your books richer because readers can connect with your writing and characters more fully.

Takeaway: Don't lose sight of the many benefits that come from planning a series.

Series that Intersect

Question: How would you go about planning several series that take place in the same world?

Answer: This is a simple question, but the answer is multifaceted.

If you're planning several series that take place in the same world, there are three considerations.

Standalone Series: If one series won't intersect with the other but shares the same world, then you can outline each series separately, as if each were a standalone series. This process is straightforward.

Intersecting Series: If the series will intersect, start with a simple series outline for each series. Factor into it the characters and the timeline.

Since I assume you won't work in more than one series at the same time—from a marketing standpoint, I'd advise against it—the next step is to make a book outline for each book in the first series. Again, note the characters in each book and the timeline.

As you deviate from your outline when you write, update your outline with this new information. This step is critical, because you'll need these details for consistency and continuity when you write the other series. Document everything. Don't trust your memory.

Also, will the same characters appear in multiple series? This is a delightful occurrence for readers, but it's a perplexing dilemma for creators because it requires detailed planning and attention to detail.

Document the personality, description, and backstory for each of your characters. Each character will also need a timeline, so they don't appear in different places at the same time in different series. For example, we shouldn't have a person stranded on an island in a book from series one and on a yacht circumventing the world at the same time in another series. Don't depend on your memory to recall these details—which you might not need for several years—as you move from one series to the next.

Multiple Authors: If different authors will write in different series, then you need to provide each author with the initial details about the world. This information will help each series stay consistent with the other ones. And if a writer adds a detail to the world that no one has yet defined, then you need a way to share this detail with the other writers.

For example, let's say the original information about the world contains no mention of it having a moon. If one writer needs the planet to have a moon, make sure the other writers are aware of it. This effort will keep a third writer from talking about the planet having twin moons or no moons, which will frustrate readers who read both series.

This undertaking can get confusing fast and is hard to manage—even more so when multiple authors are involved. Documentation and communication are key.

Summary: Regardless of whether you're writing all the series yourself or involving other writers, pursue two intents: the first is the need for detailed planning and the second is careful and up-to-date documentation. And if multiple writers are involved, you need a way to communicate this information to everyone.

Writing multiple series in the same world is a grand undertaking with the potential for great rewards.

Takeaway: The larger a project's scope, the more planning and documentation required.

4. Getting Feedback

As writers, we all need feedback on our work prior to publication. Editors help tremendously, but preliminary advice can also come in many other forms. And these options are low-cost or even no-cost.

Since the following suggestions shouldn't replace an editor, use these ideas first. Then hire an editor to fine-tune your work.

Tips on Getting and Receiving Feedback

Question: *You once said the most important thing you did to become a better writer was to write every day. What's the second most important?*

Answer: I can easily make a list of several things, but to come up with the *one* thing to list second is more challenging. I also suppose my answer will change over time, that the one thing from a few years ago is different from today and will change again in a few years.

Given this, however, the second most valuable step I did to improve as a writer was to get feedback on my work. It was scary at first (and sometimes still is). Most of this advice comes from critique groups, but I also use beta readers and paid professionals. This last category carries a cost but is invaluable.

Keep in mind that reactions from our family and friends don't count. They love us and will only tell us good stuff. Or even worse, they'll say our writing is good when it isn't.

Instead, seek feedback from serious writers and readers. But don't request input from someone who doesn't read in your genre or nonfiction area. Make sure the people you pick to provide advice are qualified to give valuable suggestions.

Here are some ideas to get feedback:

- Join a critique group, either online or in person.

- Work with another writer to provide feedback to each other.

- Hire an editor or find a mentor to help you hone your words.

Regardless of the source, the key is figuring out which feedback to apply, which to adapt, and which to dismiss. Don't feel obligated to follow every recommendation. Each piece of advice is nothing more than one person's opinion, and that opinion may not be right for your vision of your work.

Our mission as writers is to figure out the difference between good and not-so-good advice and handle it appropriately.

Last, something that's important to me when I give and receive feedback is to "speak truth in love." I've worked with some editors who provided good suggestions, but their delivery was so caustic it made me ill.

Takeaway: Receiving feedback on our writing is critical.

FINDING A WRITING MENTOR

Question: *How can I find someone who will mentor me in my writing?*

Answer: Many writers wish they had a mentor. Even several decades after publishing my first article, I still do.

The problem is the people who are most qualified to mentor are also the busiest, and the people who have time often lack experience.

If you find someone who would make a great mentor, just ask them, but leave them room to say "no," because there's a high chance they will. They're just too busy. As an option, offer to provide them with something of value in return. It could be money, but more valuable might be a service you could offer in exchange for mentoring. If you're flexible and willing to give them something in return, the answer might turn into a "yes!" (See "Alternatives to Hiring an Editor" in chapter 5 for some creative ideas.)

Another possibility is to find someone to co-mentor. If you're both at the same place in your writing but have different strengths and weaknesses, then you can help each other grow as writers. This opportunity may be a more viable option.

Last, someone can mentor you from afar. I read some blogs and listen to many podcasts about writing and publishing. These people mentor me, even though we've never met, and most don't know me.

Takeaway: If you can't find an in-person mentor, seek creative alternatives.

Beta Reader Questions

Question: When working with beta readers, what questions do you ask them?

Answer: Congratulations on getting your book to the point of seeking feedback from beta readers.

Once you've written and self-edited your book, you're ready to seek input from beta readers. Setting expectations with beta readers is critical, or else the feedback you get may not be helpful.

Here are the three questions I ask:

    1. What parts did you like?

    2. What parts confused you?

    3. What parts bored you?

The first question lets us know what passages *not* to change. Having this knowledge is critical.

Identifying confusing sections is also important. If even one beta reader is confused, many more readers will be confused later.

The third question is also insightful. Boring passages will cause readers to stop reading. We might never get them back. Be sure to fix all the boring parts. This may require rewriting, replacing, or deleting.

If beta readers answer these three questions, they provide much valuable information.

One other item about beta readers: Some writers send their work to several beta readers at once, while others send it out sequentially, applying feedback from the first reader before sending it to the second. The first approach is faster. The second approach will help you craft a better book.

In all this discussion, the key is to get feedback. Then discern what feedback to follow and what to disregard. Doing so is essential. Don't do everything your beta readers suggest. Only do what makes sense to you.

Takeaway: Tell beta readers what you expect, and they'll provide you with valuable insights.

How to Find a Critique Group

Question: *How do I find a critique group? What if there are none where I live?*

Answer: I hear this lament a lot.

Finding a critique group is challenging. Finding one that's a good fit is even harder.

First, know that there may be some in your area, but you haven't found them yet. Keep looking. Assuming you want a local group, ask area writers if they have any suggestions. Check with bookstores (start with independents), colleges, libraries, and coffee shops—any place where writers hang out—to see if they know of any groups. Ask every writer you meet if they're aware of any area critique group. Also search online.

As an alternative, you can always start your own. That's what I did, and it wasn't hard. Look online for recommendations on leading a successful writers critique group. For my group, I merged many of the steps I found online.

Third, in lieu of local meetings, consider an online group. Just do a search for *online writing critique groups*. You'll find millions of matches. The benefit of online groups is they don't have a geographic limit and may not have a meeting time, which allows members to participate according to each person's schedule.

Whether in person or online, each group has different goals and various formats, so look them over to find one that's right for you. If your first choice isn't a good fit or the group isn't working for you, bow out and find another one. Don't waste time in the wrong group.

Takeaway: If you can't find a critique group, start one.

CRITIQUE GROUP CHARACTERISTICS

Question: *What should I look for in a critique group?*

Answer: Some critique groups can be good, some are okay, and some do harm. Here's what's important:

- The members are writers.

- The members read.

- The members balance criticism with praise. Too much of either is bad.

- The members wisely curtail feedback on pieces in genres or areas they aren't familiar with.

- The members challenge each other to improve.

- The members provide encouragement.

- The members commit to help each other.

Also, look at the leader. Is the leader effective in maintaining focus and structure? If not, the group will veer off-topic and waste time.

Takeaway: Not all critique groups are the same. Seek one that's a good fit.

5. EDITING

Editing is an unpopular topic for many writers. Some attempt to rush through it and others accept it as necessary, but evil.

First, I don't mind self-editing. In fact, I enjoy it, because I know my book is moving forward and getting closer to publication.

Second, working with an editor is a valuable process I relish—if I'm working with the right editor.

Self-Editing Tips

Question: As hard as I try to catch errors in my book, I still miss a lot. Any suggestions?

Answer: I feel your pain. Do I ever feel your pain. It's hard to catch mistakes in our own writing.

No matter how hard I try, I still miss a lot. With every piece I get back from an editor, I'm dismayed over the errors I didn't catch, even though I know better. Of course, they also spot mistakes I would have never caught, which is why I always use at least two editors for every book. Despite these shortcomings, editors often remark that my writing is clean. But given all their corrections, I'd hate to see a piece that *wasn't*.

So how do we catch errors in our writing before sending it to an editor?

Edit from a printed copy: Many authors print their work and edit from a hard copy. One author says she touches the tip of her pen to each word as she reads it. Though this is a clever idea, I don't have that much patience.

I don't print my work. I'm too frugal (codename for cheap) and environmentally conscious to waste paper and ink printing each book multiple times. Therefore, I do all my editing onscreen, knowing I'd catch more errors if I scrutinized it in printed form as opposed to an electronic version.

Read Backwards: Though it seems nonsensical, I've heard writers who insist they read backwards when proofing their work. I tried it—for about ten seconds—and gave up. I don't get this technique, not at all.

Read Aloud: To combat my aversion to printing my work, I began reading it out loud. Though my wife gave me strange looks and mocked me, I caught many more errors with this approach. Unfortunately, since I knew what I intended to write, that's often what I read, even though that's not what I typed.

Use Text-to-Speech Software: An even more effective way to proof work is through text-to-speech software. That way my computer reads my words to me. I catch so many errors this way. It may be why editors often say my writing is clean. This method works for me and works well.

I use this approach when editing my work. I do so three times for each book. The first is before it goes to my developmental editor. The second is before it goes to my copy editor/proofreader. And the third is just before I publish it.

Takeaway: Try text-to-speech software to catch errors in your writing.

ALTERNATIVES TO HIRING AN EDITOR

Question: *Short of hiring someone to edit my writing, what tips do you have to help me edit my work more effectively?*

Answer: Self-editing is hard for all writers. We know what we meant to write, so that's what we see when we try to edit our work. That's why hiring a professional editor—and not your friend who majored in English—is so critical to publishing success.

Some people, however, say they can't afford an editor, but I say you can't afford not to hire one. No one can.

Nevertheless, here are some options for the cash-starved writer:

Beginning Editor: Seek a beginning editor who wants to edit but has no finished projects to show people. The first-time editor might be willing to edit your work for free or at a reduced rate just to have something in their portfolio. Remember, every editor must have a first project to get a second one. But the first project is hard to land. You can help them as they help you.

College Writing Department: Contact the writing department at a nearby college. They might have a promising student looking for experience.

Co-Edit: Another idea is to find another writer and agree to edit each other's work. Of course, this functions best if you ask each other to edit the same amount of writing. Mutual trust is key. Strive to ensure that both parties benefit.

Exchange Services: Another creative approach is to provide a non-writing service in exchange for editing. One resourceful writer offered to clean her editor's house as payment for editing her books. You may not be into housecleaning, but look at your skill set outside of writing. What about lawn service, home-cooked meals, car repair, or babysitting? See what you can offer to someone in exchange for their editing services.

Offer Resources: Beyond exchanging services, you can share tangible items in lieu of payment (not that I have any of these resources to offer). Ideas include letting your editor stay at your vacation home or timeshare, allowing them to hunt or snowmobile on your property, or loaning them your pop-up camper or motorhome. Get creative.

Don't Ask Family and Friends: What you should avoid is asking family and friends to edit your work for free. First, free is never a significant reward. Second, with free, you get what you pay for. Third, your family and friends love you and want to see you succeed. They'll struggle to make the critical comments that all writing deserves if it's to become great writing.

Warning: Except for the co-editing option, don't rely on an editor who isn't skilled. Just because someone likes to read doesn't make them qualified. These people may make good beta readers, but don't ask them to edit. Also, having majored in English is not enough—unless their education included training on editing. Though an English major is a common path to becoming an editor, it's insufficient by itself.

Takeaway: There are many creative ways to compensate an editor.

Editing Guide

Question: I need a complete reference on punctuation and formatting. What do you suggest?

Answer: *The Elements of Style* is an excellent writing resource. Start with it. Then build on that foundation.

For a comprehensive reference on punctuation and formatting, there are several notable resources. Unfortunately, none of them are in complete agreement, with obvious conflicts. Each guide has their advocates. And many have specific applications.

While some people know the major style guides and their differences, I struggle to comprehend one. I selected *The Chicago Manual of Style* because it best addresses the various types of writing I do. I use it as my go-to reference. I also like editors who follow it. It comes in book form and is also online at www.chicagomanualofstyle.org.

In addition to *The Chicago Manual of Style* (CMS), other style guides include:

- AP (Associated Press)

- MLA (Modern Language Association)

- Turabian, often used for academic work

Special application style guides include:

- APA (American Psychological Association)

- AMA, the American Medical Association

- NLM, the National Library of Medicine

- CSE, the Council of Science Editors Manual

- ACS, the American Chemical Society

- ASA, the American Sociological Association

- The Bluebook, for the legal profession

Takeaway: *The Chicago Manual of Style* is a great resource for writers.

TYPES OF EDITORS

Question: *What skills does an editor need?*

Answer: You ask a simple question, but there isn't a simple answer.

There are three basic types of editors (and they each have various names), with each requiring a different skill set.

Developmental editor: Sometimes called a comprehensive editor, a developmental editor looks at big picture issues. For fiction, they address story arc, character development, writing voice, and plot issues. For nonfiction, the editor looks at theme, organization, structure, and writing consistency.

A developmental editor must have knowledge of your genre and the publishing industry.

Copy editor: This person looks at sentence structure and the flow between sentences, paragraphs, and chapters. They'll identify awkward passages and poor phrasing. They may point out inconsistencies and possible factual errors for you to check.

A copy editor needs to know the genre. Having a college English degree may help, especially if it includes training in editing, but a more beneficial characteristic is having taught writing and graded a lot of papers. Even better is experience in a career that requires a lot of editing.

Proofreader: A proofreader looks at details: word usage, punctuation, and grammar. This includes spelling and typos. A proofreader should enjoy specificity and be able to focus. A proofreader must know and follow a style guide, such as *The Chicago Manual of Style* (CMS).

Some proofreaders know multiple style guides, but others specialize in one and only take jobs that use that guide. The key requirement is having mastered a style guide and knowing how to apply it.

Final Thoughts: No one can do all three types of editing in one pass—nor should they. And many editors specialize in one type of editing.

The ultimate editor qualification is having successfully done the work.

Takeaway: There are three types of editors for three types of editing. Experience is key.

EDITOR PET PEEVES

Question: I know that in your work you edit a lot of content. What are some of your pet peeves?

Answer: I like this question. It gives me a chance to vent a bit.

Much of the content I edit comes from newer or untrained writers. Here are some common mistakes I often see:

- They don't spell-check their work. This step is so easy to do. Why do they skip it?

- They use "creative formatting" of their text, with **bold**, *italics*, underlines, and ***combinations*** thereof. And don't get me started on using different colored fonts. Yep, it happens. Along with this irritation is UPPER CASE text. I need to undo all these formatting issues before I can work on their submission.

- They use multiple exclamation points and question marks, sometimes in combination, to end a sentence. Use just one, but only when it's appropriate. And before adding an exclamation point, consider whether it belongs there or if a period is better. Most people overuse exclamation points. When in doubt, use a period.

- They slap something together and assume I'll fix their

mistakes. That's lazy, and sometimes it's more work than I have time to do, so I reject their submission.

- They send a draft and ask me to let them know what changes they should make. Their job is to send me their best work and not expect me to do it for them. And if they have doubts about their writing, then they're not ready to submit it.

- They request feedback. While I understand their desire for input, it should come from other sources, and not a person who expects to read a finished piece. (From a practical sense, whenever I've tried to give feedback, it's never gone well. So even when I want to help someone who asks for assistance, I know from experience not to try.)

- They miss deadlines. Sometimes we can't help needing more time, but too often it's a result of poor planning and a lack of priority. Besides, it's disrespectful. Without deadlines, nothing would ever be published.

I'm more than willing to overlook a few of these mistakes and be extra tolerant of new writers, but when these issues occur too frequently, it's often easier to reject the submission. Some writers persist in making these errors with each submission, and I groan when I see their email.

But there are other writers whose submissions I look forward to receiving. Their writing is clean and complete. I need to do little additional work to prepare it for publication.

Strive to be that kind of writer.

Takeaway: Be a writer editors love.

Finding an Editor or Proofreader

Question: Are there companies that edit or proofread books?

Answer: Maybe. Probably. But your best option is to go with a freelance editor. There are many quality professionals available to edit your work. Here are some ways to find them:

Search Online: You can do an online search for editors and wade through the responses. This method is time consuming.

Ask Other Writers: A better idea is to ask others in the writing community for recommendations. This approach will give you a vetted editor. But many authors are reluctant to share the names of their publishing team for fear these independent contractors will become too busy with new business to continue to work for them.

Editor Groups: Another useful source is editor associations and groups. They can connect you with a good editor. Sometimes they'll give you a list, and other times a real person will provide the names of editors who best meet your criteria.

Networking: Find an editor through networking. I've made many great contacts at writers conferences.

Online Resources: Finally, consider online resources. I've used Reedsy to find relevant writing professionals. I've also used Fiverr to locate freelancers. Another option is Upwork (the merger of eLance and oDesk). I've not used them recently, but I did use eLance several years ago with good results. And though I've never used it for this purpose, don't dismiss LinkedIn.

Takeaway: There are many ways to find a great editor.

6. Building a Platform

The word platform fills most writers with dread. It does for me. I've never met a writer who liked building their platform, but we all need one so we can grow a following and sell our books.

Some writers dislike platform building, and others admit to wasting time on it when they should be writing. Two common platform topics are social media and blogging.

A Place for Platform

Question: *Do I really need a platform?*

Answer: Gee, you're slowly uncovering all my blunders as a writer. Goodness knows I've made a lot of them. I suspect number three on my list of errors is that I became preoccupied with my platform.

An author platform is a tool we use to promote our books to potential readers. Platform building starts with a website and an email list. It can also include social media, networking, and public speaking. The bigger our platform, the more books we can sell, and the more likely publishers will want to work with us.

Based on a thoughtless comment from an agent who decided not to represent me because "you have no platform," I became fixated on growing my author platform. (He should have said, "you have a small platform," which was true. I would have accepted that assessment, but to say I had "no platform" after years of working on it was like a knife plunged into my heart.)

So began an unhealthy platform-building obsession. It nearly ruined my career and almost destroyed me as an author. I lost the joy of writing and was ready to give up—all because of platform.

It wasn't until I stopped fixating on growing my platform that my passion to write returned.

Having said that, I still work to grow my platform. This is a never-ending quest for all writers, as our platform could always be bigger. But I'm not putting an unhealthy amount of pressure on myself. I do what I can and don't fret (too much) over the results.

Takeaway: Though building a platform is important, writing books is critical.

Social Media Strategy

Question: How does social media fit into building my author platform?

Answer: At one time, publishers were impressed with social media quantity, such as the number of Facebook likes, Twitter followers, and so forth. But now their focus is on engagement.

Are you interacting with your social media followers and fans? Do you try to connect with them on social media? Do they appreciate the value of your posts and tweets?

On social media, follow or like the people who share your mindset. And don't worry about those who don't.

And *never* buy likes or followers. This technique accomplishes nothing positive and will cause problems. Don't focus on your number of social media connections but on the quality of interaction with the connections you do have.

But in the end, you'll find that social media does little to sell books organically (that is, without paid advertising), so only be on social media if you enjoy it.

Takeaway: On social media, focus on quality over quantity.

SOCIAL MEDIA CONTENT

Question: *What should my social media strategy be?*

Answer: Some writers post new material on social media. Others repeat content from their blog. I do neither. Here's why.

Republishing the whole post isn't a wise idea because it repeats content, and search engines dismiss duplicate content. And I feel it's too time consuming and therefore not a smart use of my time to write new material just for social media.

My goal is to direct people from social media to my website, my home base, which I own and control. Therefore, I post an *excerpt* from my blog posts on social media, such as Facebook and LinkedIn, with a link pointing back to the post on my website. I do so on Twitter, too, because their character limit necessitates brevity.

Though social media platforms prefer you to not post links—because they want to keep visitors on their site—I want to get people to *my* site. That's what's most important to me. So I tease the post on social media and send people to my site to read the full piece.

Takeaway: Use social media to send people to your website or blog.

THE PURPOSE OF BLOGGING

Question: Why should I blog? Do I have to?

Answer: Blogging serves three purposes.

Skill Enhancing: First, blogging can help us improve as a writer, train us to meet deadlines, and encourage us to write regularly. Blogging helps us get better as writers—and we all want to improve.

Platform Building: The second benefit is that blogging can help us grow our platform. This is most notable for nonfiction. (Successful blogging is harder for fiction authors. See "The Fiction Author's Blog" in chapter 7.) All publishers want us to have a nice platform. Platform is even more important for indie (self-published) authors. Of course, you can choose from many platform-building strategies, and blogging is just one of them.

Enjoyment: The important takeaway is don't blog just because someone tells you to. Blog if you enjoy it (the third benefit), can sustain it, and want to realize at least one of the first two benefits.

We'll address blogging in the next two chapters.

Takeaway: Blogging helps us improve as writers.

7. Blogging

Blogging is a common way for writers to grow their following and build their platform, which is essential for selling books. This strategy applies regardless of whether we are traditionally published or indie published.

In addition, blogging is a great way to test new material, interact with readers (assuming you allow comments and respond to them), and develop as a writer.

Blogging Expectations

Question: *As a writer, do I have to have a blog?*

Answer: I've written over 5,000 blog posts—mostly for myself, but also more for my freelance writing clients—so it may surprise you that I don't feel writers have to have a blog.

Don't blog if you:

- Don't have the time.

- Lack incentive.

- Fear it will drain you.

- Aren't willing to commit.

- Don't have enough ideas of what to write.

Blogging isn't right for everyone. If it's not right for you, invest your time and creativity elsewhere. Only pursue blogging it you *want* to blog and have ideas for posts that align with your author brand. Otherwise, don't do it.

Know that some publishers and agents will insist you blog. But if you know it's not right for you, don't let them force you into doing something you don't want to do. Walk away and look for a publisher or agent that doesn't take such a hard line.

Now, if you're still interested in blogging, let's discuss it further.

Fiction Bloggers: For fiction writers to build a following with a blog is hard, but possible. (See "The Fiction Author's Blog," later in this chapter.)

Nonfiction Bloggers: Nonfiction authors have an easier time with blogging. Just blog about the same topics you cover in your books. Build an audience around your content, and they'll be interested in your books too. (More on this in a bit.)

Alternatives to Starting a Blog: Instead of starting your own blog, you can look to guest post on other people's blogs.

Takeaway: Don't blog unless you want to.

Discover What to Blog About

Question: How do I go about starting my own blog?

Answer: A lot of writers wonder about this, so you're not alone. There are two parts to blogging: the technical aspect and the content aspect. Let's look at the content part first.

Find Your Focus: If you write whatever you feel like writing about (as I did when I started), you will never sustain an audience. Pick one topic as your blog's focus. Then go to the next step.

Brainstorm Ideas: With your blog topic or focus determined, brainstorm for ideas. Don't stop until you hit at least twenty. You may not use them all, but at least you know you have plenty of ideas to write about. If you can't come up with twenty, then you'll struggle to sustain your blog, so search for another topic.

Prewrite Five Posts: Before you even set up your blog, write your first five posts. Plan to launch your blog with several posts already there.

Schedule Time: You should post once a week (and no less frequently than monthly. How long did it take to write each of your posts? Do you have enough time every week to devote to it?

Moving forward: If you still want to blog, you can move forward with the technical aspects of setting up your blog, which we'll cover in chapter 8, "Blogging with WordPress."

Takeaway: Your blog should focus on one topic or area.

BLOG YOUR BOOK

Question: *I've heard about writers "blogging their book" before publishing it, to draw attention to it. What are your thoughts?*

Answer: Yes, some writers "blog their book" before publishing it to draw attention to it. But if you do, will people buy your book? Opinions differ on this strategy. Here are my thoughts.

Yes, some people blog their book (often part of it, but usually not everything) before publishing it. The posts serve to draw readers into the topic and then point readers to their book.

I've yet to hear anyone who felt their blog posts hurt book sales. Even when their entire book is available on their blog, they still think their posts help sales, not hurt them. It comes down to convenience. A book is easier to read than clicking through a series of posts on a website. Also, the purpose of blogs is for short, intermittent reading, while books have the opposite goal.

There's one caveat. If all or much of your book is posted online, some book sellers my see this and flag your book as derivative or even plagiarized. Then it's up to you to convince them it's your content that you hold the rights to.

Other people turn blog posts into a book (see "Book Your Blog"). I've blogged parts of several books in advance of writing them—including this one.

Blogging your book and booking your blog works great with nonfiction and even memoir, but it's difficult to pull off for fiction (see "The Fiction Author's Blog"). Fiction writers can't dole out their novel in blog-sized chunks. Of course, exceptions exist, but they're rare.

Takeaway: You can blog your book.

BOOK YOUR BLOG

Question: What about "booking my blog," or turning blog posts into a book?

Answer: Some people claim you can't sell anything you've offered for free. They assume you can't charge for something you once gave away (and may still be giving away) on your blog. An agent or publisher may also be concerned, fearful there will be no one left to sell to.

I disagree.

Even if you've blogged the entire book and it's available for free, authors have had success selling the same information in book form. Though you may have lost some sales, you will pick up a new audience with a book. In addition, some of your blog readers will buy a copy because they want all the content in one place in a convenient format, while others who read some posts won't read the rest online, though they will read your book. Although it's best if you can add new content to the book that isn't in your blog, this recommendation isn't a requirement.

There are many cases of authors who had success turning a series of blog posts—or even one post—into a book. With all the indie-publishing options available to us today, I say go for it: book your blog.

Takeaway: You can turn your blog posts into a book.

The Fiction Author's Blog

Question: Blogging makes sense for nonfiction writers, but I write fiction. What should I blog about?

Answer: While the content vision is clear for nonfiction blogging, it's murky when it comes to fiction.

With fiction, we can't blog excerpts from our book because we will either end up posting the entire book or leave readers frustrated over gaps in the story. Besides, who wants to read an entire book in blog-length passages, spread over several months?

This doesn't mean fiction writers can't connect their blog with their book. Though I've not done any blogging for my novels, here are some ideas to consider:

Blog about the Era: If your novel takes place in a different time, be it past or future, blog about the period. For historical settings, you've already researched this era thoroughly, so post what you've learned. For futuristic novels, share details about the world you created.

Blog about the Location: If the story takes place in another country—or another world—give details about the setting.

Share Deleted Scenes: Just as movie DVDs often have deleted scenes, your book may have scenes you didn't use. Share these pieces with your fans. Do they wish the deleted scene had stayed in the book? The one caution is if you want to save the unused scenes for another book.

Disclose Character Bios: Many novelists write character profiles for the protagonist and antagonist, as well as for supporting characters. Since only some of these details make it into your book, you can share the complete profile on your blog.

Reveal Backstory: Often there is background information, which, although interesting, doesn't move the story forward and isn't suitable for a book. Blogging unused backstory is a way to engage readers and build excitement for your book.

Post Short Stories about Your Characters: Have you ever finished a book and wanted to read more about the main character? Or discover more about an interesting, but ancillary, side character? Short stories can fill that need in readers, building interest in the book without revealing too much.

Final Thoughts: The timing on when to post these ideas varies. Some function well as pre-publication buildup, whereas others lend themselves to post-publication promotion.

The key is that fiction writers can support their book through a blog. It just requires a bit more creativity.

Takeaway: Fiction authors can blog, too, but it's a bit trickier.

Writing a Book versus Blogging

Question: I want to write a book, and I want to blog. Which should I do?

Answer: I'm glad you're thinking about this. Many writers try to blog and write a book at the same time. They end up doing neither one well. Or they try to write a book before they're ready. Then they end up with something not suitable for publication, waste a lot of time, and endure much frustration. That assumes they finish the book. But they're more apt to give up before they finish—because they're not yet ready to write a book.

Unless you've done a lot of writing—say about one million words—and invested about 10,000 hours honing your skill (see "10,000 Hours" in chapter 1), I recommend you start with blogging or writing short articles, essays, or flash fiction. Blogging (and short pieces) offer several advantages:

- Blog posts are quick and easy to write.

- Blogging is a great way to hone our writing skills and find our voice.

- Feedback is fast.

- Errors are easy to fix.

- Bloggers develop a habit of writing regularly, even when they don't feel like it.

- Blogging according to a schedule—which is what all bloggers should do—trains us to meet deadlines.

- Blogging prepares us to write longer pieces.

There are many other benefits associated with blogging, but these outcomes are some of the key ones, which is why I recommend starting out with blogging or writing other short pieces. Save the book for later (see "Work Up to Writing a Book," in chapter 2).

Takeaway: Beginning writers may want to start with blogging (or writing short pieces) and save their book for later.

8. Blogging with WordPress

In addition to my love for blogging, I'm a huge advocate of WordPress as the go-to tool for setting up and managing blogs and websites. WordPress currently powers about 43 percent of all websites worldwide, far outdistancing its next competitor. And their market share is growing.

Though other blogging options exist, WordPress is a proven platform, backed with support from its parent company (Automattic) and its passionate community of enthusiasts.

That's why whenever someone asks me what blogging or website platform I recommend, I always say WordPress.

WORDPRESS.COM VERSUS WORDPRESS.ORG

Question: I understand WordPress has two versions: hosted and self-hosted. Serious writers recommend self-hosting. As a beginner I'm considering starting with the hosted version. How easy is it to switch once I get comfortable with blogging?

Answer: You ask an astute question. But before I answer, here is some background:

The hosted version of WordPress (WordPress.com) is easy to learn and use. It also has minimal features. The self-hosted version of WordPress (WordPress.org) is flexible and feature-rich, but it has a steeper learning curve.

Like most people, I recommend any author serious about their website and blogging use the self-hosted version, WordPress.org, and bypass the hosted version, WordPress.com. But that may not be the right approach for you—at least not at the start.

WordPress.com: WordPress.com is simpler and cheaper (approaching free) to set up and use, but it doesn't have as many features or as much flexibility. Just go to WordPress.com and click on "Get Started." You can get a basic site up and running in a few hours.

For a person not sure about blogging and who wants to try it out, Wordpress.com will work fine with minimal fuss and no cost. Though I've seen some successful authors use a WordPress.com-powered website, it always surprises me. Yes, you can have many of the elements of a professional site using WordPress.com, but it will always have a basic appearance.

WordPress.org: If you have the time and the interest, you can develop a smart, professional-looking site by yourself and for little cost using wordpress.org (the self-hosted option), which is why I advocate it.

WordPress.org is far more powerful, but it's also more involved to set up. In addition, this option comes with costs: buying a domain name (an annual fee) and paying for hosting (a monthly fee).

Go to WordPress.org, click "Get WordPress," and follow all the steps, focusing on the parts about getting a host. Be patient and allow yourself time to read and understand it. Setting up a site on WordPress.org won't be as fast as WordPress.com, but the results will be worth it.

As an alternative, many developers will design a WordPress website for you and even host and maintain it, but the costs add up. If the thought of doing a WordPress.org website yourself overwhelms you or if you don't want to invest the time and money, then focus on making your WordPress.com site as good as you can.

Moving Content: A related issue is if you start with WordPress.com and want to switch to WordPress.org. Moving content from one to the other isn't hard. Transferring posts is as simple as following a short set of steps. There are a lot of instructions online to help you transfer content from WordPress.com to WordPress.org.

Takeaway: You can't go wrong with WordPress for your website and blog.

USING BLOG CATEGORIES

Question: *How helpful is it to set up categories in my blog?*

Answer: With WordPress, think of your website or blog as a file cabinet and categories as drawers in the file cabinet, which allow you to group related content together.

Here are the purposes for blog categories:

Search Engine Optimization: One use of blog categories is for search engine optimization (SEO), which allows the search engines to better find and index your posts.

Reader Engagement: The second use of blog categories is to help readers find similar content. For example, if we blog about three subtopics and a reader is only interested in one of them, they can click on the category and see just those posts.

Writer Organization: A third benefit of using blog categories is to help us in our own organization.

Here are two examples: I once tweaked the focus on one of my blogs, and some of the old posts no longer fit my new vision. Since I had these old posts in one category, it was easy to find and remove them.

In another instance I decided to write a book using some blog posts. Again, they were all in one category, which made them easy to find and access.

Here are some other items about categories:

- Having one category offers no benefit.

- Having too many categories is confusing. Aim to have three to eight categories.

- Using the default of "uncategorized" is unprofessional and accomplishes nothing.

A Final Point: Don't confuse categories with tags. They seem similar but have different applications. We'll cover them next.

Takeaway: Use WordPress categories to group similar content together.

Using Blog Tags

Question: *What's the difference between categories and tags? Don't they do the same thing?*

Answer: Though tags and categories seem the same, they are different.

View a tag as a cross-reference tool. Tags can be a subset of a category (like a folder in a file cabinet drawer), transcend categories (like an index), or both. Regardless, their purpose is to link related content.

Every post needs at least one tag and can have more, but don't go crazy. One or two is great, more is okay, but stop at six.

In determining tags, consider recurring themes or words in your posts. Unlike categories, you don't need to limit the number of tags you use, but do seek tags you can reuse. A tag used once accomplishes nothing.

Takeaway: Use WordPress tags to link related posts.

REMOVING ADS FROM WORDPRESS.COM SITES

Question: My website is through wordpress.com. WordPress puts ads on my website. Is there anything I can do about this?

Answer: Though ads that automatically appear on WordPress.com sites are frustrating, it's a reasonable trade-off for a free website. While some readers will overlook the ads, others won't, detracting from their reader experience. Another concern is displaying ads for products and services you might not like, appreciate, or agree with. (Note that WordPress.org sites do *not* display ads.)

As part of their business plan, WordPress.com places advertising on your site so they can offset the cost of offering it to you for free. If you upgrade to a Premium plan, they will remove the ads and provide extra features.

Or you can switch to WordPress.org. Then enjoy even more features, greater control over your website, and no ads. Moving takes extra work and incurs an added expense, but for many people, switching is worth it for all the added features and control.

If mastering WordPress.org daunts you, the WordPress community is helpful in answering questions and simplifying the learning curve. The most challenging step is the first one: finding a host and getting set up. (Check out "WordPress.com versus WordPress.org," earlier in this chapter, for more information.)

Takeaway: There are options to remove ads from your WordPress.com site.

SEO Tips and Tricks

Question: I hear a lot about SEO (search engine optimization). Should I be concerned about keywords?

Answer: That's a great question, one with two answers. If you're talking about using the keyword metatag, don't worry about it. Google says they ignore it and so do most search engines, so don't waste any time thinking about metatag keywords.

But if you're talking about keywords or keyword phrases to guide your writing and include in your text, this is something I encourage you to pursue if you're interested in SEO.

SEO is part art and part science.

It includes coming up with keywords or key phrases. It takes time to develop this skill. There are many books, blogs, and podcasts that explain SEO. In addition, SEO best practices continually evolve.

Not to oversimplify a complex topic, a reasonable starting point is to consider what words you would type in a search engine to find the post you're writing. Then use this phrase repeatedly—without getting carried away—in the post's text.

Last, try to include this word or phrase in your SEO title, SEO description, the alt text for your graphic, and the URL (web address) for the post. If these details make your brain spin, don't worry about them now. As you learn more about blogging and SEO, they'll begin to make sense.

Takeaway: Pursue SEO for your website or blog, but don't let it overwhelm you.

9. Submit Your Work

Though a few people write for themselves and no one else, most writers long to share their work with others, even if they have a bit of fear in doing so. This usually means submitting their work for publication.

These questions address the art and angst of submitting our work.

How to Format Your Submission

Question: How should I format my writing before I submit it?

Answer: There are two main points for proper formatting.

First, follow the common basic criteria that most everyone agrees on. I'll share this in a moment.

Second, most publishers and editors will tell you what *else* they expect (if anything) in their submission guidelines. So follow the basic formatting expectations in all your work, and tweak it as needed for specific instances.

The Basics: Here are the basics:

- Times New Roman font: 12 point, black

- Double-spacing between lines

- One space after the end of a sentence

- Flush left and jagged right (that is, left justified but not right)

- One half inch paragraph indentations (not five spaces or a tab)

- One-inch top and bottom margins

- Equal side margins (either one inch or one and a half inches)

- No hard breaks (that is, a "carriage return") at the end of each line

- No extra lines at the end of a paragraph, except for a scene break or transition.

- A docx Microsoft Word file (not the old doc format)

If you follow these basic tips, few editors will object, and most will consider you a pro.

Bonus Tips: Here are some bonus tips:

- Don't use different margin settings on odd and even pages (as you would see in a book).

- On the first page, include your name and contact information (email, phone, and mailing address) at the top, along with the word count (and with articles and short stories, indicate the rights you're offering). Some publications will specify placing this information at the top right and others, the top left. Some will say to put these details in the header, and others will specify the top of page one, so expect some variation, but the key is to not omit this information.

- For all other pages, add a header with your last name, short title, and the page number. There may be some variations on this requirement too, but the main goal is to have this key information in a header (or footer), not on the page itself.

Don't Panic: Don't let formatting paralyze you. Editors will overlook a minor deviation or two without complaint. Most editors want you to succeed. Read that again: Most editors want you to succeed.

Following conventional formatting—along with great writing—will help get your work noticed and published.

Takeaway: Follow basic formatting expectations to give your submission the best chance for success.

GENERAL SUBMISSION TIPS

Question: What are some general submission guidelines that apply in most all situations?

Answer: Based on my experience as a magazine publisher, here are my suggestions for submitting your work for publication. These apply regardless of what you're submitting or where you're submitting it:

Know the Publisher, Publication, or Website: The first step is to familiarize yourself with your submission target. Look at the type of content they publish, its length, the style used, and its tone. Strive to match these characteristics.

As you read their past content, see if your idea fits. If not, don't force it. Seek a different topic or a different outlet.

Look for Submission Guidelines: Find their submission guidelines on their website. Publishers and publications that accept unsolicited submissions post their expectations. Read and follow their guidelines precisely.

If they don't have their submission guidelines posted, it's doubtful they accept unsolicited submissions. Though you could email (or even call) to find out, you're more apt to irritate them. Accept that you may not get a response. Also, never email them with a submission question until you've scoured their website for an answer.

Write the Best Possible Piece You Can: You know the drill: write, rewrite, edit, spell-check, and proofread. Ask a trusted writer to review it before you submit it. You get one chance with this piece at this publication.

Note that some publishers don't want to see a finished piece. Instead, they may want you to pitch your idea first. They could prefer a formal proposal, a summary, an abstract, or a blurb. If they specify this requirement, don't dismiss it.

Follow Their Requirements with Care: Reread their submission guidelines and meet every expectation. Then send it without further delay in the manner they specify. Though most editors won't disqualify your piece for making a tiny blunder, it could count against you, and too many errors will result in a rejection.

Be Patient: Some publications acknowledge submissions, and others don't. If they say they do and you haven't heard back in a few weeks (or months, for books) ask—politely. If they accept your piece, be patient. It can take a while for them to post it online and several months or more for print. And books take much longer.

Thank Them: Most writers skip this step. Don't be one of them. Once they publish your piece, thank them—even if some aspect wasn't to your satisfaction. If you have an idea for another piece, idea, or book—or are open to receive an assignment—now is the ideal time to mention it.

Follow these tips and you'll submit like a pro, which will move you ahead of most writers.

Takeaway: Submit your work like a professional.

PERIODICAL SUBMISSION TIPS

Question: How do I go about submitting content to publications and blogs?

Answer: In addition to the generic guidelines in "General Submission Tips," here are three specific considerations for submitting to periodicals, as well as blogs. I list them from least important to most important, but if you don't get past the first one, you'll never get to the second. And you must pass the second step to have your writing considered.

Make Sure Your Submissions Match What the Periodical Publishes: For example, my publications address niche industries. I want relevant trade articles. Over the years I've had people submit short stories, poems, song lyrics, and even a recipe. They never bothered to see what content I publish. As a result, they wasted my time and theirs.

Pay attention to the content they publish, the length of the articles, stories, or posts, and the writing tone. Strive to match those characteristics.

Follow the Submission Guidelines: Periodicals list their guidelines for two reasons: first, to allow the periodical editor to work more effectively and second, so the writer can present their work in the most favorable light.

The guidelines are there for your benefit, to help you and not constrain you.

Also, for blogs, know that not all blogs accept guest posts. They may state this information on their website, or you may need to search their archives to find out.

Submit Your Best Possible Work: Even though your submission will undergo editing—which happens to every piece, regardless of who wrote it—make it the best you can. Proofread it carefully, spell-check it, and ensure it says what you want it to say. Then email it. Don't delay.

Move Forward: Follow these three keys to maximize your chance for acceptance.

Takeaway: Doing your homework before writing and submitting will save time, lessen disappointment, and reduce rejection.

Query Letters and Book Proposals

Question: What's the difference between a query letter and a book proposal?

Answer: Early in my career, I thought a query and a proposal were two names for the same document. Boy, was I confused.

A query letter is a short communication to get an agent or publisher's attention. If your query letter succeeds, they'll ask for a book proposal. A proposal is a lengthy, detailed document that shares key elements of your book in organized sections. If they like your proposal, they'll ask to see the full book (for fiction) or encourage you to move forward in writing the book (for nonfiction).

The Query Letter: There's a lot of information online about writing a query letter. Unfortunately, there's disagreement over what to do. It's as much art as science. Despite differing opinions on the specific content and order, here are the pointers I've picked up and use:

- Address it to a specific agent, following the agent's guidelines and making sure they accept queries in your genre.

- Open with a concise connection to the agent (sincere and non-embellished), followed by a great hook, sell your idea, and then sell yourself (including your platform). This should take four paragraphs. Making it longer makes it too long.

- Keep it to one normal page (even though you will email it as text).

- Don't ask them to click a link or download an attachment. I understand most will skip your link and few will download an attachment unless they know you and requested that you attach a document.

- Keep it professional. Avoid being cute, clever, or gimmicky.

- Spell-check and proofread carefully.

Note that in the non-book world, some periodical and online publishers also want you to query them first. Others just want to see the finished work. If they ask for a query, the preceding discussion applies.

A One Sheet: Something like a query letter is a one sheet (sometimes called a one-pager). It's a document that you might hand to an interested agent or publisher whom you meet at a writing conference. It contains much the same information as a query, but can include more, as much as comfortably fits on one page. A one sheet can also include relevant graphics and professional formatting, which you should avoid in a straight-text query letter.

A Book Proposal: Whether you have a fiction or nonfiction book, agents and publishers who like your query letter will expect you to send a book proposal next, even if the book is complete. There are many courses and books that teach how to draft a book proposal, so I won't try to cram all this information into a brief overview.

Do an online search, and you'll receive more matches than you have time to read. Unfortunately, not everyone agrees with the expectations for a book proposal, and some contradict each other. Focus on recommendations from successful agents and authors who have sold a lot of books to traditional publishers. You will benefit from their experience.

Here are the sections I include in my nonfiction book proposals:

- book title

- synopsis

- hook

- target audience

- table of contents

- detailed outline

- about the author

- author platform

- competitive titles

- sample chapters

Though I've never done a fiction book proposal, the sections are about the same. The main difference is that, instead of including a chapter-by-chapter detailed outline, a fiction proposal needs a concise summary of the entire book, including any spoilers. Don't hold back. Condense your book into a couple of pages.

Search online for specific examples of nonfiction and fiction book proposals to further guide your work on your own proposal.

Make the best proposal you can. Some agents and publishers will tell you what they expect in a book proposal. Follow their instructions exactly.

If your proposal follows their format, it's easier for them to evaluate. And if it doesn't meet their expectations, it's easier for them to reject, because they know you're a person who won't follow directions or doesn't think the instructions apply. You will be a challenging writer to work with. No one wants that.

Takeaway: To pursue a traditional publisher, master the art of writing compelling queries, one sheets, and proposals.

SUBMISSION FEEDBACK

Question: Why don't editors, agents, and publishers give feedback when they reject a submission?

Answer: Editors, agents, and publishers rarely give feedback when they reject a submission. As a writer I share your frustration—deeply. As a publisher I know the reason why.

After trying in vain to give authors feedback and wasting way too much time in the process, I've given up. I can better spend my time working with the submissions I accept to make them the best they can be.

When I reject a submission, it's with a short message: "I have decided to pass. Sorry." This response is curt, but anything more, such as to tell them why, spirals into a series of email exchanges that are time consuming and unproductive.

Few people who ask me for feedback want to improve. Instead, they hope to change my mind.

If a person submits something outside the type of content my publication uses, I delete their message. This action may seem harsh, yet they didn't even bother to read the submission guidelines and don't have a clue what I publish. I owe them nothing.

I get many unsolicited submissions each day, along with many more spam emails. Sometimes it's hard to tell the difference. Seriously. If it takes too much time to wade through a too-long text, I hit delete. I, like every other publisher, editor, and agent, have limited time. I need to make every minute count.

Instead of hoping for submission feedback, use other resources to improve as a writer. (See chapter 4, "Getting Feedback.") Then submit your best work according to the submission guidelines. That's what I do.

And if you happen to receive feedback, thank the sender and seriously consider what they shared. But don't view this as an invitation for ongoing interaction—unless they explicitly state that.

Takeaway: If you receive feedback on your submission, treat it as a valued gift.

COMMON SUBMISSION ERRORS

Question: What are the biggest mistakes people make when submitting content for publication?

Answer: That's a great question, but it's hard to answer. I'll share the top mistakes I see writers make when submitting their work:

Not Following Submission Guidelines: The first submission error is not following directions. Adhering to submission guidelines helps increase the chance of them publishing your work. Each deviation lessens the likelihood of success.

Common mistakes include missing deadlines (a huge no-no), submitting content not accepted by the publication, and having a piece that's the wrong length. Too many writers ignore the directions for submissions.

Not Proofreading Their Work: The second submission mistake is not proofreading their submission. Most editors will overlook an error or two, but when it's clear that the author never even ran spell-check, it's obvious they haven't bothered to send their best work, and they expect the editor to clean it up.

Not Adhering to Writing Conventions: The third submission error is using non-standard formatting. Some writers must think creative formatting equals creative writing. It does not. They use odd fonts or switch fonts within the piece, various point sizes, multiple colors, and lots of bold, italics, <u>underline</u>, **all three**, and ALL CAPS.

All these formatting issues require work to clean up. Make it simple for editors by submitting clean copy with no embellished formatting.

Takeaway: You make your writing stand out when you avoid common submission errors.

10. AGENTS

A literary agent serves as an intermediary between author and publisher. They represent authors and present their queries and book proposals to publishers. If the publisher wants to publish the book, the agent negotiates the best possible deal for the author, their client.

Agents only make money when their authors make money, so they're selective in who they sign.

WHEN YOU NEED AN AGENT

Question: *Do I need an agent?*

Answer: If you hope to publish your book with a traditional publisher, you'll need an agent. Most publishers—except for some small ones—only work with agents.

Even if you find a publisher who will work with you directly, you should still use an agent. Why?

Because an agent will negotiate a better contract than you could do on your own. Even if you are a lawyer or know one (who works outside of the publishing industry), an agent understands the publishing industry and is in a better position to get you the best possible deal.

Of course, if you plan to indie publish, there is no need for an agent.

Takeaway: Traditional publishers expect you to have an agent.

Tips on Finding an Agent

Question: *I'm frustrated. How do I go about finding an agent?*

Answer: Finding an agent is easy. Just do an online search for "literary agents." But getting an agent to agree to represent you is hard.

Unlike hiring an accountant or attorney, where we can vet them and pick the best one to meet our needs, agents vet their clients (authors) so *they* can pick the best ones.

Remember, agents only earn money if they sell one of their clients' books. So unless a client is a great writer with a compelling idea, there's a good chance the agent will spend a lot of time working for the client and have nothing to show for it. Therefore, they have a strong incentive to only take on clients whose work they think they can sell.

This reality means writers need to sell themselves to agents. Here's what's required:

- Hone your skill as a writer.

- Set up a professional author website. Agents will look for one and expect to find it.

- If you're on social media, make sure it's professional and presents you in a positive manner. Do everything you can to remove negative posts and unflattering photos—though you should have never posted them in the first place. Remember, once something's online, it never truly goes away.

- Study how to pitch your book, write a one-page summary, submit a query, and produce a book proposal.

- Learn about agents you'd like to have represent you. Follow their blogs and make respectful, thoughtful comments. But don't annoy them.

- Ask writers you trust to give you an honest answer if your work is ready for agents.

Know that writing ability is only part of the equation. Agents will also want you to have a platform so you can help sell books. (See chapter 6, "Building a Platform.") When I was looking for an agent, one agent declined to represent me, not because of my writing, but because he said I didn't have a platform. Ouch!

A final item is to be patient. Finding an agent to represent you takes time: several months and often years. As you wait, keep working to improve as a writer and building your platform.

Takeaway: Finding an agent takes time and finding one who's a good match takes even longer, so be patient.

WHAT AGENTS HANDLE

Question: *Do agents handle shorter pieces, such as articles, short stories, or poems?*

Answer: I'd love an agent who would handle shorter pieces. Unfortunately, I've never heard of one who does. They only deal in book-length projects.

Agents earn a commission on projects sold. The payoff for shorter pieces is too small for them to spend time pitching. They need to invest their time on bigger works that pay better.

Takeaway: Work directly with publishers for shorter pieces.

11. PUBLISHING

For people to read our work, we need to publish it. Here are some thoughts to help you move forward to publish your work.

PUBLISHING OPTIONS

Question: Should I go with a traditional publisher or self-publish my book?

Answer: Writers often struggle over this. I understand what they're asking, but permit me to rephrase it. The question should be: Should I indie publish or *pursue* a traditional publisher?

We have no control over whether a traditional publisher will want to publish our book. What we can control is *pursuing* a traditional publishing deal.

For most writers, I don't recommend trying to find a traditional publisher. (See the next question, "Traditional Publishing.") That leaves self-publishing, also called indie publishing.

I recommend the book *Successful Self-Publishing* by Joanna Penn. Do everything she says, and you'll be ahead of most people. Expect indie publishing to cost a minimum of $1,000 to $2,000 per book, but it can go much higher. Most of this cost goes for a professional cover and editing. And if you want an audio book, too, the cost will easily double.

Bonus Tip: Joanna Penn has written many books to help writers on their journey. I recommend them all.

Takeaway: You can publish your book yourself or *pursue* a traditional publishing deal.

Traditional Publishing

Question: I just want to write, should I pursue traditional publishing?

Answer: Landing a traditional publishing deal is harder now than ever before. Publishers are risk adverse and require you to have an effective platform to promote and sell books. And most traditional publishers won't interact with authors. They require you to have an agent. Finding an agent takes time.

Remember, an agent only makes money when they land a publishing deal for their client. Therefore, agents only take on an author if the agent thinks they can sell the author's work. (Read more in chapter 10, "Agents.")

Again, having a platform to move books is key for both agents and publishers. (See chapter 6, "Building a Platform.") Additionally, agents are interested in authors who will write many books.

Though it's never been harder to land a traditional publishing deal, there have never been more opportunities for indie publishing.

Takeaway: Landing a traditional publishing deal is hard and takes time.

Indie Publishing Versus Traditional Publishing

Question: *With so many self-publishing options out there, why should I bother to pursue a traditional publisher for my book?*

Answer: I love this question!

Here are the pros and cons of indie publishing versus going with a traditional publisher:

Traditional Publishing Pros and Cons: In most cases, traditional publishing requires less of the author, should result in more book sales over a wider distribution, and carries the prestige of a publisher selecting your book for publication. The negatives include the effort to find a publisher, the length of time to publish the book, and earning much less per copy sold—if anything at all.

Indie Publishing Pros and Cons: If you're self-disciplined, indie publishing allows you to get your book to market faster. You also maintain full control over the final product and make more on each sale. The downside is that you must view publishing as a business and cover all the costs of producing the book yourself.

A commonly cited reason to not indie publish is the requirement to market and promote our books. While it's true that if we indie publish, we must market our books if we hope to sell any, traditional publishers also expect us to help promote, market, and sell our books. If you can't or won't do that, the publisher is apt to pass on publishing your book.

In short, they want authors who can move product.

Conclusion: There is no right answer to the issue of indie publishing versus pursuing a traditional book deal. It depends on the goals and priorities of each author. Also, some authors do both, depending on the book. They're hybrid authors, going with traditional publishers for some books and indie publishing others.

Takeaway: Pursue the publishing approach that's right for you.

Book Support Services

Question: Is there a company that guides you through the process of writing a book, from initial writing to publishing?

Answer: Yes, there are companies and individuals who will guide a writer through the process of writing a book, from initial writing to publishing.

Just do an online search for *book writing consultants* or *book writing services*. You'll get hundreds of millions of matches. But I wouldn't take this route. Here's why.

On the low end of the price range, you may just get a list of steps to take. But don't pay someone for this information because I'm going to list the steps in just a bit. (See the next question, "Indie Publishing Checklist.")

On the high end of the price range—at thousands or even tens of thousands of dollars—you get someone who will hold your hand and advise you every step of the way. They may even do some steps for you. If you have more money than time, try this approach, though I'm confident the results won't be much better than if you follow my list.

Takeaway: Don't hire someone to do what you can do yourself.

INDIE PUBLISHING CHECKLIST

Question: *I'm overwhelmed by all that's involved in indie publishing. Do you have a list of what to do?*

Answer: Here are the key steps to write and indie publish a book.

1. Develop your initial concept and vision. This step includes market research into competitive titles to gauge the book's marketability.

2. Write the first draft for the entire book.

3. Do your first edits. Continue to fine-tune until you feel you're ready for feedback.

4. Run spell and grammar check.

5. Get feedback from beta readers or critique groups and fine-tune your book, though this step can also happen after step eight.

6. Run spell and grammar check, again.

7. Get a developmental edit. Some people call this edit a book critique, while others call it a substantial edit. But these labels can also refer to different services. What you want is

big-picture feedback. At this stage, you need someone to give you an overview of the strengths and weaknesses of your book. They should address how it flows, its overall arc, and identify anything that's out of place, missing, or not needed. You also want someone to point out shortcomings in your writing style—we all have them, but we can't see them until someone tells us.

8. Incorporate the feedback of your developmental edit, as appropriate, into your book. Evaluate every recommendation, but don't feel you need to accept each one. When you feel you've implemented all the *relevant* changes, proceed to the next step.

9. Run spell and grammar check, a third time.

10. Have someone copy edit your book. This edit looks at writing at the sentence level.

11. Again, discerning what advice to follow and what to dismiss, make the needed changes.

12. Have someone proofread your book. This edit addresses grammar and punctuation. It focuses on details. Though many authors separate copy editing and proofreading into two steps, most of the editors I work with do both at the same time. This saves money and shaves weeks off the publishing timeline.

13. Make a final read through of the book yourself. Since you've already had professionals review your book, make changes with great care at this point. If in doubt, leave it as is.

14. Format your book for epub (the format needed for e-books). I do this formatting myself using a free online tool. There are many out there. Just ask around to find the current preferences.

15. Once you've formatted your e-book, verify that everything looks the way you want it to.

16. Concurrent to the copy edit and proofread phases, design your book cover. Unless you have graphic software and the skill to produce a cover equal to or better than traditional publishers, hire a cover designer.

17. Upload your e-book to your publisher or publishing aggregator or both. (An aggregator is a company that sends your book to many outlets. Upload it once to them, and they send it out for you.) Though an incomplete list, these are the publishing outlets I use:

    ○ Amazon, to reach the US audience, you must be on Amazon

    ○ Kobo, which is great for other countries, such as Canada

    ○ Google Play, which can also do auto-narrated audiobooks.

    ○ Draft2Digital, a publishing aggregator

    ○ Publish Drive, a publishing aggregator

18. If you want to do a paperback version, which I recommend, do the interior layout. The required format is a PDF file. There are also tools to do this, though most have a cost involved. You can

also hire someone to do this for you.

19. Verify that everything in your PDF is correct.

20. Upload your paperback version to your publisher or publishers. These are the ones I use:

   ○ Amazon

   ○ IngramSpark

21. Now it's time to launch and market your book. Marketing gives us a whole new topic to deal with, which we'll cover in the next chapter.

Since I've written and published many books, I made my own checklist (on which the above list is based) to make sure I cover everything and don't miss a step. As more options become available and I learn more about the writing and publishing process, I continue to fine-tune my list. If you plan on being a multi-book author, I suggest you make your own checklist too.

Takeaway: Follow a publishing checklist to make sure you cover everything.

ASSISTED PUBLISHING

Question: *Who do you use to self-publish?*

Answer: To self-publish—or indie-publish—you do it yourself. You don't go through someone else.

Assisted publishing or subsidy publishing is paying a company (or a person) to publish your book for you. I don't have any experience using assisted publishing because it's not the right option for me, nor is it the right option for most authors.

If you go this route, check references, ask a lot of questions, and treat it like a business decision—because it is. Some companies are good, some are not, and some are rip-offs. I've heard rates from several hundred dollars to tens of thousands. And that's a lot of money to pay for something you can do yourself if you indie publish your book.

Now, my statement about doing everything yourself if you indie publish is an oversimplification. In truth, we hire experts to handle various aspects for us. In this way we act like a general contractor on a building project.

For example, I hire editors and cover designers. I coordinate their work to move toward a finished project: a published book. This approach is very much a business process.

Whichever publishing option you pick, I wish you the best.

Takeaway: Indie publishing involves hiring independent contractors to handle specialized tasks. With assisted publishing, you pay someone to do all this for you.

E-BOOK FORMATTING

Question: *What are your thoughts on formatting e-books? How important is it to have a professionally looking format for e-books? What do you do?*

Answer: This is an interesting question. I format my own e-books. For me, it's a matter of control.

With more people indie publishing and many doing their own formatting, readers don't expect one ideal format. Even traditional publishers aren't consistent in how they format their e-books. The key is to make sure the formatting doesn't get in the way of the reader experience.

Over the years, I've used various free e-book formatting tools. I output an epub file and test it. I continue to tweak it until I'm satisfied with the results. When it's good, I upload it to the various online bookstores and book aggregators.

For authors who don't want to mess with e-book formatting, you can hire someone to do it for you. Just ask other authors who they use. Also check out Reedsy and Fiverr. I've used both for publishing-related services and had positive experiences.

Takeaway: You can format your e-book yourself or outsource it.

ISBNs

Question: Can you help me understand the benefits of purchasing an ISBN?

Answer: Many indie authors don't use ISBNs for their e-books, and they see no reason why they should. The number Amazon and other sellers provide works just fine from a practical standpoint.

But an ISBN gives your book added credibility and has more universal recognition than an ASIN (Amazon Standard Identification Number) when searching for a book by number. So I opt for an ISBN.

In most cases, ISBNs cost money. Each country has their own way of assigning ISBNs and with differing costs—from free to expensive. You'll need one ISBN for each format your book is in: hardcover, paperback, e-book, audio, and large print. So that's five ISBNs for each book.

ISBNs are more important for print books. ISBNs facilitate ordering and tracking. Though bookstores won't deal with indie-published authors (unless you are local or have a connection with the manager), the book needs an ISBN for bookstores to order and track it.

Some companies will provide a free ISBN as part of their services. Scrutinize what rights you may give up when you use their ISBN. Since I want to remain in control of my books and content, I always opt to buy my own ISBNs.

Takeaway: Getting an ISBN is a best practice for your e-book and a requirement for your print book.

AUDIOBOOKS

Question: Do I need to publish an audiobook?

Answer: Audiobooks are the fastest-growing segment of the publishing industry. Demand for audiobooks will continue to grow and will remain strong. But audiobooks are also expensive to produce, much more so than e-books and print books.

So before jumping on the audiobook bandwagon, authors should proceed with care. It can be a huge investment that takes a long time to produce a return, if at all.

Some successful indie authors have worked out revenue-share agreements with book narrators, where the narrator doesn't charge anything up front and agrees to split sales revenue, often 50-50. But narrators only make these revenue-share agreements with authors who have a history of selling books. Therefore, this option is unavailable for many writers.

This means if we want to have an audiobook, we need to pay the production costs ourselves. This price can be several hundred dollars per finished hour of audio. And though the author will keep 100 percent of the book sales, they also take on all the financial risk.

But technology stands poised to revolutionize audiobook production. Already, tools exist that can produce a near-perfect text-to-speech rendition of a book using artificial intelligence (AI). But currently, most book retailers prohibit the sale of these automated productions. I'm confident this will change.

Even more exciting is the future possibility of a computer being able to cost-effectively sample our voice and then produce a narrated book that sounds like us. I don't know how soon this change will happen, but it will occur, and it may be soon.

Personally, I'd love to have all my books in audio, but it's not a good business decision for me right now. But that will change, and when it does, I'll produce audio versions of all my books.

Takeaway: There is much potential in audiobooks.

12. MARKETING

Regardless whether we indie publish our book or go with a traditional publisher, we must take the lead in marketing if we hope for it to be successful.

This falls squarely on the shoulders of the indie-published author. Yet book marketing has also become an expectation for traditionally published authors, as well. Only A-list authors can get by without marketing their books.

For every other published author, marketing is a requirement.

Book Marketability Basics

Question: I don't want to spend time writing a book that isn't marketable. What are some basic guidelines?

Answer: Let's start with some general principles of what types of books are not marketable. Though exceptions exist, they are rare:

- A book that's too long or too short for its genre

- A book of poetry, unless you're famous

- Your autobiography, unless you're famous or infamous

- A book of short stories, unless you're an established fiction author

- A nonfiction book for which you have no authority or credentials

- A topic of personal suffering that many others have already covered

In addition to these items, don't chase trends. It takes about two years to have a book traditionally published, so by the time you write your trendy piece, the trend could have ended, and no one will want your book. You also risk it seeming derivative.

Also, never write in a genre (fiction) or a topic (nonfiction) that doesn't fire your passion. You'll find it boring to write, and readers will find it boring to read. Instead, find something you're passionate about. And then write it.

Takeaway: Learn basic genre expectations before you start writing.

How to Know If a Book is Marketable

Question: Is there anyone I could pay to get an opinion on what's marketable before I spend hours writing?

Answer: You can do an internet search to find someone to hire to tell you if your book is marketable, but I recommend going to the websites of agents you respect. Some provide writer services on the side and would be glad to charge you a fee to offer their opinion. Other agent sites provide lists of respected service providers.

But the operative word here is *opinion*. Aside from some basic traps to avoid, which we covered in "Book Marketability Basics," the best anyone can do is offer their opinion. Ask two people, and you'll get two opinions.

Consider all the accounts we hear about agents and editors rejecting submissions based on their opinion that the book won't sell. But then after twenty, forty, or even more rejections, it crosses one person's desk, and she doesn't reject it. She thinks it's marketable. Sometimes this prediction proves correct, and the book becomes a best seller.

You can ask around and even pay for advice, but in the end, you might be further ahead to go with your gut and write what you're passionate about.

Takeaway: Remember that someone's opinion of your book is exactly that: an opinion.

WRITING ABOUT YOUR HEALTH SCARE

Question: Will publishers be interested in my book about my health scare that almost killed me?

Answer: Your story is very personal for you, very real and raw. Unfortunately, it isn't unique. And publishers want unique books—unless you have a big platform to move books. Then they don't care so much about your topic because your celebrity status will overcome it.

Publishers interested in your topic already have one or more books on the subject, and taking on another one could hurt the sales of the books they already have, so they'll pass.

And publishers who haven't published a book on your topic haven't done so because they're not interested in the subject.

The one possible scenario is a publisher who has published a book on your topic, but it's dated or not selling well. Then they may look to replace it with a new book—providing you have a platform to move books and an agent to represent you.

Takeaway: Just because a book idea is significant to you, doesn't mean it's marketable.

Using an Advance for Marketing

Question: *I've signed with the publisher and, aside from a disappointingly low advance, they strongly suggested that I use my advance to market my book. Though this sounds reasonable, it doesn't sit well with me. What are your thoughts?*

Answer: I agree that it sounds reasonable, but my advice is not to do it unless you have a long-term reason for it.

First, let's talk about advances. An advance for a book was originally intended as money for the author to live on as they wrote their book.

Nowadays, fiction books must be completed before a publisher offers a contract. Many nonfiction authors also write their book before signing a publishing agreement. Therefore, needing an advance to cover living expenses while writing the book is no longer an issue.

Over time the advances have reportedly decreased to the mid to low four figures. I even know of one publisher who routinely offers $100 advances, though I do question their ethics.

Though you are understandably disappointed about your low advance, it's not unusual.

This brings us to your publisher's request to use your meager advance to market your book. The worry is that if your first book doesn't sell well, they'll never offer a contract for your second one. Spending your advance to market your first book to ensure a second book is published may be a move you want to make. Just know that the second book contract is not guaranteed.

Consider, however, the reality of book publishing. Most traditionally published books don't earn out. This means there's never enough book sales to offset the advance. Therefore, the writer never earns one penny of royalties.

As a result, for most traditionally published authors, the advance is the only money they'll ever earn from their book. Though you may be an exception to this, the odds are that you won't.

Do you really want to spend all your book's earnings on marketing?

Take away: Though there is no right answer, consider carefully how you use your book advance.

HIRING MARKETING EXPERTS

Question: I don't want to market my books. Can I hire someone to do this for me?

Answer: Hiring someone to market our books seems like a logical decision. After all, we hire professionals to edit our books and design our covers, so why not book marketing too?

This is exactly what I thought and precisely what I did. Over the years I've hired a book launch expert, a publicist, a book marketing consultant, and an SEO (search engine optimization) guru, a social media specialist, and a book marketing professional.

Each one was a complete failure. I was never able to directly attribute a single book sale to the tens of thousands of dollars I spent hiring them. Nor did I ever see an overall bump in book sales during their time with me.

The only hire that came close to working out was the book ads expert. After three months of losses, the fourth month generated more attributable book sales than ad costs. Yet once I paid the fee for their services, I still lost money.

Now I run my own ads. I also do all the other needed book marketing activities—even though I don't want to.

Takeaway: Though authors can hire professionals to cover many areas, finding an effective book marketer may not be one of them.

Do-It-Yourself Marketing

Question: If I must market my own books, what tips do you have so that it won't drive me crazy?

Answer: After several years of unsuccessfully hiring book marketing experts, I realized I had two choices. The first was to not do any book promotion. The other was to do it myself.

With great reticence, I decided to do it myself. I did this knowing it would detract from my writing and reduce my output.

I looked at the conventional book promotion strategies of traditional book publishers, all the while suspecting that much of it no longer applies in today's rapidly changing publishing landscape. I made a list. Next, I added what leading indie-published authors were doing. Some of the items seem doable and others turned my stomach; just thinking about them made me nauseous.

Then I divided the list into three categories: the *yes* list, the *maybe* list, and the *no* list.

My *yes* list included all the marketing I was open to do. The second list of *maybe* items contained activities I was willing to do if needed. And the final list, which contained my *no* tasks, were things I was unwilling to do, my non negotiables.

With clarity in place, I set about developing a book marketing strategy that would tap into my *yes* list and avoid my *no* list. It's what works for me, and it may work for you.

Takeaway: Do the book marketing activities you're willing to do and avoid the ones that suck the life out of you. This won't maximize book sales, but it will keep you moving forward in a healthy way for the long term.

13. Legal Stuff

Many people have questions about the legal aspects of writing and publishing. As I address these concerns, remember: I'm not a lawyer, and I'm not giving legal advice. I'm sharing my opinion.

An excellent resource is Helen Sedwick's book *Self-Publisher's Legal Handbook*. This book stands as an essential tool every writer should read, study, and follow.

PROTECT BLOG CONTENT

Question: *Is it necessary or wise to protect content you write in a blog? What if it is material for other writing projects? Should it be freely accessible online? I have not heard anyone address this.*

Answer: You're in good company. Writers often wonder about copyrights and protecting their blog content.

To start, place a copyright notice on your website and blog. This notification will help keep honest people honest, and it lets readers know you're serious about your work. But beyond that, it accomplishes little else.

In the United States, our work enjoys an automatic copyright as soon as we produce it. Though for additional protection, a best practice is to also register the copyright for books. We'll cover that topic in a bit in "Register My Copyright."

If you're concerned with people copying your work, that is, stealing it, there is always a chance it could happen. Though the risk is small, there's nothing you can do to prevent it—short of not blogging—so the best solution is to not worry about it and post what you want to post.

If the posts will be part of a future book—something many people have done—you might want to hold back some content, but bloggers who've blogged their entire nonfiction book—and even fiction book—didn't feel it hurt sales. (See "Blog your Book" and "Book

Your Blog," in chapter 7.)

If the posts are from your traditionally published book, check with your publisher. They may not want you to post anything from your book, and depending on your contract, it may be illegal to do so.

Takeaway: Take reasonable steps to protect your work, but don't fixate on it.

Copyright Registration

Question: I know that my writing is automatically copyrighted as soon as I write it, so is there any need to register the copyright?

Answer: Registering a copyright for a book is a best practice for a career author and helps protect our intellectual property, a key asset for authors. Registering our copyright provides a stronger legal footing if anyone ever disputes ownership or authorship of our work. Additionally, a registered copyright is essential in the event of a lawsuit. (Though it's possible to register a copyright for blog posts, other short works, and even unpublished content, doing so is expensive and cumbersome to manage.)

Beyond that, in the United States, the copyright lasts for seventy years after the death of the author, so registering our copyright helps our heirs to better earn money from our intellectual property (our writing) after we're gone.

Registering your copyright is not hard, but it might look foreboding, especially the first time. In the United States, go to www.copyright.gov. Though most of the application process is straightforward, beware that a couple of areas could trip you up. Therefore, I recommend taking a class or going through a tutorial first.

Though registering the copyright for my first book took a couple of hours, I can now complete a registration in about fifteen minutes. This small investment will protect my book, both during my lifetime and for my heirs.

(This discussion about copyright and registration relates to the United States. Other countries have different copyright laws and registration processes.)

Takeaway: Be sure to register your book's copyright.

GDPR

Question: *What's the deal with GDPR. Do I need to make changes to how I collect emails on my website?*

Answer: That's a huge question. Here are my thoughts.

As it applies to writers, the GDPR (General Data Protection Regulation) affects us if we have people from the European Union on our mailing list and even if they visit our website.

Some people outside of Europe chose to remove all European subscribers from their mailing list, and others decided to ignore the law. Both are extreme responses.

As I understand it, the two main points that apply to us as writers are that when someone from the European Union gives us their email address, we must be clear what we will do with it, such as add them to our email newsletter list or send them periodic updates. Second, if they unsubscribe, we must stop emailing them immediately.

Email marketing providers comply with GDPR, and they tell us what changes we need to do on our part to follow this law. Key steps include updating the wording on our opt-in message and our privacy statement on our website. GDPR also applies to BookFunnel and other providers that gather email addresses for us.

Some people think we need to provide notice on our website for visitors from the European Union if our website uses cookies (most do), and that we must have all people from Europe (and unknown locations) resubscribe to our mailing list.

Others predict that GDPR will emerge as a best practice that we should all follow. But the short answer for those not in the European Union, when it comes to GDPR, is to do what your email marketing provider recommends. For those in the European Union, consult legal resources in your country for additional steps.

Takeaway: Don't ignore GDPR and do as your email marketing provider instructs.

Selling Full Rights

Question: A publisher is interested in some devotionals I wrote. They pay an honorarium of $35 per item, and then they want full rights forever. Is this typical? Is it fair?

Answer: I don't think anyone can make decent money writing devotionals. They do it for other reasons.

Some periodical publishers pay a small fee or honorarium to authors. Though they often ask for full rights for a limited time, others want full rights forever. To many authors, this doesn't seem right or fair.

I earned $15 each for some short pieces I wrote several years ago. They wanted full rights for one year after publication. Now the rights have reverted to me. Another publication paid $60 per piece, also with a one-year stipulation. In both cases, their payment was too low, but I wanted to see my work in their publication.

In another case, I sold full rights in perpetuity for some teen devotionals for $30 each, but it wasn't for the money. Though they were fast to write, by the time I finished several rounds of edits to make them just right, I suspect I made minimum wage for my efforts.

Unless I have a strategic reason, I never give anyone exclusive rights in perpetuity. One reason I might is to say my work appeared in a prestigious publication, but I would never sell them something I wanted to use elsewhere.

Unfortunately, payments this small are typical. Fairness is another issue. It boils down to this: are you willing to give up your words forever for a few bucks?

Takeaway: Use caution and consider the ramifications before selling all rights to your work.

Including Images and Photos

Question: What about using images and photos I find online for my blog or book?

Answer: Using photos, images, and clip art in a book or blog post is a dicey issue. Just because you found it online, doesn't mean it's free or legal to use. Don't do it.

Only use work that states something like "Royalty free for commercial use."

In addition to that, you can do a reverse image search: Just upload the image in question, and they'll check their index to see if anyone claims ownership.

If it's okay to use, keep a record of the results, and then consult a couple more sites just to be sure. (Do an online search for *reverse image search engines* for other options.)

If it's not legally permissible for you to use, then buy a royalty-free license (not an editorial license) or find alternative artwork. If you buy a non-exclusive license, then others can use the image as well. A more expensive exclusive license means only you can use it.

For my blog I only use sites that contain artwork that is legal for me to use. There are both free and paid sites. For book covers, my designers only use legally permitted and properly licensed artwork.

Takeaway: Make sure your blog's and book's artwork is legal to use.

CITING SOURCES FOR QUOTES

Question: Each chapter in my book starts with a quotation. Most of the quotes came from internet sites. Do I need to include a page citing where I obtained each quote?

Answer: Using quotes in a book is another legal dilemma.

For traditionally published books, your publisher will have its own requirements for you to follow. And each publisher may have a different expectation. In addition, they also have a legal team to help keep you and them out of legal trouble—or at least minimize risk.

In general, they will want you to attribute your source. I heard of one publisher who insisted on a signed release for each quote. This burdensome requirement is a good reason to not use quotations.

If you're indie publishing your book, I recommend you always cite your sources. But in my books, I try to avoid using any quotes, in any way, from any source. This approach is the surest way to minimize legal problems.

The issue gets extra messy when a quote is online. The site may have copied the quote from someone else; that is, they stole it from the original author. If you use that quote—even with citation—you then perpetuate their plagiarism, and their crime becomes your crime.

So removing quotes might be your best approach. That's what I would do.

Remember, I'm not a lawyer and this chapter does not contain legal advice. Again, I encourage you to check out Helen Sedwick's excellent book *Self-Publisher's Legal Handbook.*

Takeaway: Exercise care when including quotes in books and other writing.

14. FINANCES

Even though many authors consider themselves artists and believe that discussions of money taint their art, money is an integral part of life. As writers we will do well to embrace this reality. Though we don't need to abandon the idea of writing as art, we should accept it as part art and part business.

Book Publishing Costs

Question: How much does it cost to indie publish a book?

Answer: The price to indie publish a book varies greatly. The answer depends on your skills, budget, and book length.

I've heard people explain how you can publish a book for under one hundred dollars. While their advice is accurate, the results won't produce a professional-looking book that will get people's attention and earn good reviews. I suggest not trying to publish a book on the cheap.

There are also people who outsource much of the work and pay several thousand or even tens of thousands of dollars to publish a book. If you have a lot of money, that may be the option to choose.

For myself, I currently budget $1000-$1500 per book. Here are my typical expenses:

- Developmental Edit: $200 to $800 (though you can spend much more)

- Copy edit/Proofread: $300 to $600 (depending on the book length)

- Cover Design: $300 to $500

I do everything else myself, so the only cost there is my time.

For the developmental edit and copy edit/proofread, many editors charge by the word. Others charge by the page or by the hour. I prefer the per-word fee because I know what my cost will be. Though you can find people offshore who will do this service for much less, be careful. They may not speak English as their primary language or even if they do, their editing work may fail to meet the expectations of native English readers. Also, with any type of editing work, the longer the book, the more it will cost.

For the cover design and interior layout, you can save money by going offshore and still get a professional result. I've worked with cover designers in several countries and have gotten good quality artwork. I've only worked with one interior layout designer, and she did a great job.

Takeaway: Know what it will cost to publish a book and then budget for it.

Traditional Book Publishing Costs

Question: How much does it cost to publish a book with a traditional publisher?

Answer: Nothing. It doesn't cost a thing to go with a traditional publisher—except for your time.

That's the beauty of having a book traditionally published. It costs you nothing, and they pay you. Expect an advance and royalties once (if) your book sells enough copies to offset your advance.

A traditional publisher who wants you to pay them for any aspect of the process is either not a true traditional publisher or a scam artist. Don't pay them one cent. Either seek a true traditional publisher or publish the book yourself.

Takeaway: You should never pay a traditional publisher one penny. They pay you.

WRITE FULL-TIME

Question: *Is it possible to be a full-time writer?*

Answer: Yes. But . . .

I heard one author quip that in the United States more people earn their living from playing Major League Baseball than from being full-time novelists. Ouch! The truth is few people make their living full-time from book writing.

And most of those full-time authors earn their income from a variety of sources. For example, I write books, am a commercial freelance writer, and publish magazines and e-zines. From these three areas I earn my living as a full-time writer. Most full-time authors have a similar situation.

Though I hope to one day make my complete living through writing books—and have a plan to get there—I'm not there yet. I might never achieve that goal, but it is my dream.

Being a full-time writer is possible, but it takes patience and creativity. Also, don't expect to get rich through writing. If you happen to make a lot of money through writing, consider it a bonus. Instead, resolve to be satisfied living a simple life and able to cover your basic living expenses through writing.

Takeaway: There are many variations to the idea of writing full-time. Pick the approach that fits best for you.

FINANCIAL CONSIDERATIONS

Question: What are the financial considerations before becoming a full-time writer?

Answer: Don't quit your day job. I'm serious.

I don't know anyone who one day quit their job and transitioned into being a full-time writer the next day. It takes years to make that move.

While you still have your full-time job, start writing on the side. How much money can you generate from it? As your income from writing increases and provides consistent revenue month after month, you can consider scaling back your other job and ramping up your writing.

But before you take this step, pare back your expenses as much as possible. Beyond living simply, live frugally. Be prepared to do so for as long as necessary. Also, set aside a cash reserve to pay your bills as you make this transition.

When I switched from a traditional job to going solo, my family had no debt (not even for our house), and I had six months of income in the bank as a safety net. I used it all. I also had an emergency fund, which I didn't need.

Many authors wanting to go full-time look at their current expenses and think they need to make that much money through writing. Instead, they should look at how much they can reduce expenses. Doing so will make the transition easier.

Takeaway: Lower your living expenses as much as possible before going full-time as a writer.

FREELANCE WRITING

Question: How much can I make as a freelance writer?

Answer: Like most broad questions, it all depends.

Being a freelance writer can take many forms, some lucrative and others that leave you struggling as a pauper.

Payment for most freelance work is by the finished piece, though some might be per word. But when it comes to looking at how much you can earn as a freelancer, *always* think in terms of dollars per hour. If you charge $100 for a piece that takes you five hours to write and edit, you're earning $20 an hour.

Unless there's a strategic reason to do so, aim to make at least minimum wage for your freelance work. But don't be satisfied with that. Seek higher-paying work, knowing that the effective hourly rate for experienced freelancing can be $50, $100, or even more an hour. But use this hourly rate for analysis purposes only, and don't share it with clients. Instead quote the price per finished piece or the rate per word.

Though I've never quoted a project rate per hour, there may be times when a project is so undefined that quoting an hourly rate is the only option. But then, I just pass on those types of messy projects.

And never compete on price. That's a race to the bottom. Someone will always undercut you.

Instead, here's how to go about getting the better-paying freelance gigs.

Start by considering what you like to write and are good at. Then find a niche you're knowledgeable about—or willing to become knowledgeable about. Look at how much competition you would face in the market. Then consider what clients are willing to pay. In general, the less competition you have, the more you can charge, and the more people will pay.

For myself, I like to write blog posts and am good at it. I selected a small niche market I know well and promoted my services for writing content marketing pieces. Because of my knowledge of the industry and long-standing reputation, coupled with the ability to write fast and well, I have little competition.

As a result, I make enough income from being a commercial freelance writer in this niche market that I *could* support myself full-time through it—if needed. Fortunately, I have revenue from other sources to supplement my freelance writing.

The point is that it's possible to earn a living through freelance writing. But you need to find a niche with little or no competition and produce great content that your clients will love and pay for.

Takeaway: Be strategic to earn decent money through freelance writing.

GHOSTWRITING WORK

Question: *Someone asked me to write their book for them. They have nothing on paper. I would have to spend time with them, take notes, and then write their story. How does one charge an appropriate fee for this type of job?*

Answer: That's a great question. I've ghostwritten some books and enjoyed doing so. The payment is most always a fixed rate, paid in installments. The first payment is due before starting the project. The final payment is due when the writer submits the finished product to the author. (The person who hires you is the *author*, and you are the *writer*.)

The number of installments is up to you and the author. Two, three, or four are common, but my last book was in ten installments (per the author's request). Also, try to frontload the installments so you receive more money in the beginning. That way if the project doesn't work out, the author changes their mind, or they stop paying, then you have received just compensation for your work to date.

Don't write on spec or have it contingent on them getting a book deal. Also, avoid a revenue share based on books sold. Though you could negotiate a base fee *plus* a revenue share, unless the author has a large platform and can sell books, assume there will never be any significant revenue for them to share with you. So make your base fee large enough to make the project worthwhile. (See the next question,

"Ghostwriting Fees," for some general rate ideas.)

If you need to interview the author, such as for an autobiography or memoir, your fee should cover your time. Estimate high. You may need to help the author organize their thoughts, or they may be evasive or unwilling to share, which has happened to me.

Two related items: Always have a written agreement that states your fees, the installment amounts and dates, and details of what you will include and not include. A basic "work-for-hire" agreement should suffice. (Remember, I am not a lawyer, and this response is not legal advice.)

The other item is to be aware that you are selling your words and cannot claim them as your own or reuse them for another purpose. Though a nice author may share the byline with you or acknowledge you were the writer, most will not.

Takeaway: Start every ghostwriting project with an agreement that details your fee, payments, and what is and isn't included.

Ghostwriting Fees

Question: What fee is appropriate to charge to ghostwrite a book? Is this a good way to make a living as a writer?

Answer: I didn't know what to quote for the first book I ghostwrote and charged in the mid-four figures. It was too low, but it was a simple project, so my compensation worked out okay.

My second ghostwriting experience was more involved, and I quoted twice as much. It was still on the low side, but the fees for that book turned out okay, as well.

I understand that the minimum going rate for a ghostwriter is $15,000, with experienced ghostwriters in the $25,000 to $35,000 range. And I've heard of much higher numbers too.

Just remember, ghostwriters seldom get any recognition for their work, aside from a nice paycheck. In most cases ghostwriters won't see their name on the cover, title page, or online listings. And the ghostwriter contract will often prohibit them from telling anyone they ghostwrote the book.

Ghostwriting is great for writers who just want to write, can write fast, and don't seek recognition or acclaim for their work.

Takeaway: Ghostwriting books is a viable way to earn a living, but it's not right for everyone.

15. Other Considerations

Last, we'll tackle some remaining items that are important but don't fit in the previous chapters.

DEALING WITH REJECTION

Question: *What tips do you have for dealing with rejection?*

Answer: Rejection can come at two times: prior to publication and after publication.

Pre-publication rejection comes from agents and publishers saying "no" to our work. It isn't good enough or "doesn't meet our needs at this time." A form of what can feel like rejection also comes from feedback on our work from critique groups, beta readers, and editors.

Post-publication rejection comes from reviews and online (or in-person) criticism of our work. This type of rejection is often the hardest to deal with because it may be mean-spirited or a personal attack.

Regardless of when it occurs, here are some ways to deal with rejection and negative feedback:

Accept that Rejection Will Occur: Know that rejection and negative feedback are part of what it is to be a writer. There's no way to avoid it. The common advice is to develop a thick skin. Yes, that's true. But how do we go about becoming thick-skinned?

Developing a thick skin isn't easy, but try focusing on the reasons why you write. What drew you to writing in the first place? What parts of it give you joy or fill you with satisfaction? Hold on to these positive elements of writing when dealing with the hurt of rejection.

Some writers keep a file of positive notes, emails, and other encouraging feedback. When rejection or hurtful comments occur, they spend time reviewing what they've saved in their file to offset the negative.

Consider the Source: Look at who is rejecting or criticizing your work. Do they know what they're talking about? Do they have the expertise to state an informed opinion? Have they even read your piece, or are they rejecting what you wrote based on some external or inconsequential bit of information?

Everyone has a right to state their opinion, but not everyone's opinion is worth our time to consider it.

Seek to Learn from It: Each rejection or criticism holds the potential for a learning opportunity. Yes, rejection stings. But often there's something in it we can take hold of and use to improve our writing, whether it's in this piece or the next. Don't dismiss these potential tidbits just because they exist within a hurtful rebuke.

Know When to Dismiss It: We should ignore some rejections and criticisms outright. Negativity that fails to address our writing but instead focuses on us as an individual is a personal attack that doesn't merit our attention. Recognize that the person making this attack has a personal issue they're dealing with inappropriately. Unfortunately, they chose to direct their problem at you. Dismiss their words and move on.

Limit Your Exposure: Many authors never read the book reviews that readers post online. They face two risks in doing so. One is to believe all the five-star reviews, and the other is to believe all the one-star reviews. Both give us an unbalanced perception of our writing ability or lack thereof. Therefore, don't read your reviews.

Other authors have an assistant read their reviews. They relay only those comments that may contain relevance to the author.

Of course, pledging to not read reviews and then following through is hard. But the risk of not doing so is too high, with one scathing review—even if unwarranted—possessing the potential to send us into a downward spiral of despair.

Instead of reading reviews, write your next book.

Take Time to Grieve: This bit of advice reminds us to not push aside the pain of rejection but to acknowledge it. Just don't wallow in it. Some people take a day or two to cool off. Others indulge in a guilty pleasure, such as a bowl of ice cream or chocolate candy bar. Or they may hang out with friends who understand them, love them, and encourage them. Then they resume writing.

Any writer who shares their work with anyone should expect various forms of rejection to occur. Accept this reality as part of writing, but strive to not let it damage you as a writer or as a person. Use it to make you a better writer and a stronger person. Then keep on writing.

Takeaway: Writers face a lot of rejection and negativity, so learn how to minimize its impact.

GRAMMAR CHECKING PROGRAMS

Question: I'm looking for a grammar-checking program. Is there one you can recommend?

Answer: I once signed up for a trial of Grammarly, a most impressive grammar checker. The problem was that Grammarly flagged numerous items to review, but I lacked the needed background to comprehend many of the issues. (I missed learning grammar in elementary school and never caught up; more on that in "My Story" at the end of this book.) I couldn't understand the explanations behind many of their suggestions, so I didn't know what to change or even if I should change it.

After taking a fresh look at Grammarly, it now seems easier to use. Other writers recommend ProWritingAid. But regardless of the tool or resource we use, we must have a working knowledge of grammar to make the right choices. Though you can use either tool for both fiction and nonfiction, most writers recommend ProWritingAid for fiction and Grammarly for nonfiction. (I use ProWritingAid for both.)

The built-in grammar checker in Microsoft Word, however, is an ideal place to start. Though this approach still requires us to decide which suggestions to accept and which ones to reject, it's easier to manage. While this effort won't catch everything—and will flag some issues it shouldn't—it covers the basics.

I start with the grammar checker in Word to make a first pass. Then I move to ProWritingAid for a more in-depth look.

In my experience as a publications editor, most of the submissions I receive would benefit from doing this basic grammar check in Word before they submit their work. It seems many people have turned off this option (I once did), and some don't bother to run spell-check either. Don't make these mistakes.

Takeaway: Use a grammar checking tool before submitting or publishing your work.

Word Processing Alternatives

Question: Microsoft Word is expensive. What are some alternatives?

Answer: Yes, Microsoft Word is expensive, but it's also the de facto standard for writing and publishing. I urge you to use it. Even so, many writers seek options for word processing software, either to save money, increase functionality, or both.

As an alternative to purchasing Microsoft Word (or Office) you can check out Office 365. It includes Word, but instead of buying the software for several hundred dollars, you pay a small monthly fee. As a benefit you always have the latest version, and depending on your license, you may get to put it on multiple computers.

Scrivener, a popular writing tool designed for how writers think and work, is well-liked, especially with novelists. It costs a fraction of Microsoft Word. Scrivener, designed for writers, has powerful features that creative people crave. It can also output a docx file—an essential requirement—as well as many other formats.

Another option increasing in popularity is Google Docs. It costs nothing, and your files save online. This way you can access them from any internet-connected computer, at any time.

Regardless of the tool you use for writing, make sure it can output in Microsoft Word format (docx), because most all publishers require a Word file submission. In addition, *all* editors I've worked with in the past twenty years have used Word (except for one who edited a printout).

Regardless, Microsoft Word remains the industry standard—and my recommendation.

Takeaway: Save money on buying Microsoft Word by using Office 365.

Contest Payment Conundrum

Question: *Should I pay to enter contests?*

Answer: I've paid to enter some contests. I don't mind it when I win, but it's a double hit when I don't.

I've paid from $1 to $20, and each time they gave a compelling reason why I needed to compensate them to consider my work. And each time I've felt duped afterward.

Going forward, the only reason I'll pay to enter a contest is if I'll receive feedback on my submission. So far, I've never seen this service offered in the contests I've considered.

Also, beware of bogus contests, whose only purpose is to make money for the contest owner through the submission fees they collect. Research contests carefully, and steer clear if you have concerns.

Takeaway: Be wary of contests that charge an entry fee.

Writing Advice that May Not Be True

Question: *There is a lot of writing advice out there. Is there any commonly repeated information that I should be careful with or is just plain wrong?*

Answer: There's lots of advice floating around about writing, being a writer, and finding success. Though well-intentioned, some of this advice is bad information or oversimplified counsel. Here are some tips I've heard, many of which I've also said.

Check out these common pieces of advice and discover the truth about them. Though we've already touched on some of them, I repeat them here, so they'll appear in one place.

Show Don't Tell: Using words to paint a picture (showing) is more powerful than to state what happened (telling). In general, this tip is good advice, but it's sometimes better to just tell readers what happened. For example, it would be boring to spend several pages showing readers about a four-hour car ride where nothing significant occurs. Instead just say, "Four hours later they arrived at their destination." That's telling, and in this case it's the right approach.

Write Every Day: Yup, I said this maxim before, and I share this tip every chance I get. But I don't mean it literally. I mean it figuratively. What I mean is to write regularly. Although for you it might mean every day, it could be every weekday or only on the weekend. The point is to have a writing schedule and commit to it.

Although this guideline makes sense to me, and I wouldn't have it any other way, some writers chafe at the thought of writing every day. Instead they only write when they're inspired or have a deadline. If this idea works for you, embrace it. Ignore the advice to write every day, but not until you've tried it first.

Write in the Morning: This tip is another one of my favorite adages. Many people even claim scientific confirmation that the morning is the best time to write (or do anything important), with maximum productivity and optimum results. My morning production is far better than in the afternoon. Writing in the morning works for me and works well. The early hours are when the good stuff happens.

Some people claim the morning isn't right for them, that other times of the day work better. If that's you, and you've tried mornings only to find them lacking, ignore those of us who insist you write in the morning. Pick the time of the day that works best for you.

Write What You Know: There's an element of truth to this recommendation. What we know best, we can write most effectively.

When it comes to nonfiction, writing what I know flows with greater clarity and speed. But that doesn't mean I can't research something I don't know and write an effective piece. I've done it many times.

When it comes to fiction, if I only wrote what I knew, it would be a boring piece about a middle-aged white guy living an uneventful, routine life. Who'd want to read that? Therefore, in my fiction, I write about what I don't know. More specifically, I write what I can imagine. Then I live vicariously through my characters and their experiences that I make up.

You Must Have a Platform: An agent once rejected my submission, not because of the quality of my work or relevance of my idea, but because he deemed my platform inadequate. I doubled down and began working on building my platform in earnest. I hated it. It sapped the life from me. I almost quit writing because platform building distressed me so much.

Yes, having a platform to sell our books is important, regardless of whether we want to indie publish or hope to be traditionally published. A platform will help us be successful faster, but it isn't a requirement.

You Must Be Active on Social Media: This statement often finds itself coupled with building an author platform. I'm on several social media sites, but I don't get them—not really. And although social media is at times enjoyable, it can be a huge time suck. I'm better off spending that time writing.

Someone who enjoys social media and understands how to use it to connect with people can realize great benefits. But I'm not one of them. I connect best with others through my newsletter, on my blog, and via email.

You Must Have a Website: I agree that an author website is essential. It doesn't have to be fancy or extensive, but it must exist and be inviting.

And for writers who think social media is an acceptable alternative to a website, I vehemently disagree. A social media platform can change its rules at any time for any reason, can shut down your account without warning, or not allow your followers to see your content. These actions happen all the time.

But a website is something we control. That's why it's essential. Even so, some authors claim to get along fine without one.

You Must Have an Email List: Email isn't a sexy, new technology, but it is a proven method of reaching people. As authors, having an email list remains our most effective way of selling books. If you don't have an email list, start one today. Every name you ethically and legally add to your list is a prequalified buyer for your books. Sure, you may get by without an email list, but why risk not using the most effective book marketing tool available?

Always Use an Outline: When I write, I always have a plan to guide me. It may be an outline, bullet points, or a destination to write toward. This approach is the most effective way to write quickly, not waste words, and avoid unnecessary amounts of cutting. Using an outline is the most efficient way to write, and as a career author seeking to drive income through my words, greater efficiency means increased revenue potential.

There's nothing wrong with being a discovery writer (a pantser)—and many authors prefer this method, claiming that having a plan stifles their creativity. But this approach isn't the fastest and most efficient way to write. You decide what works best for you.

Use Microsoft Word: I've been using Microsoft Word longer than I can remember. Although I used other word processing programs before it, they're now ancient. Microsoft Word is the standard throughout the publishing industry. Although alternatives exist and each one has its merits, you'll never go wrong using what the rest of the industry uses. (See "Word Processing Alternatives," earlier in this chapter.)

You Must Use an Editor: Although this tip is wise advice, it isn't absolute. No one forces you to use an editor before you publish your work. But if you want to avoid harsh criticism and one-star reviews, use an editor. And if you say you can't afford to use one, I say you can't afford not to. Your writing career and your reputation as an author is at stake. (See chapter 5, "Editing.")

I normally use two editors for each book, sometimes more. I can guarantee you they don't catch everything—no book is error-free—but they do make my work a whole lot better than I could have ever done on my own.

Don't Design Your Own Book Cover: Again, no one makes you hire a cover designer for your book. You can do it yourself. But unless you have experience as a graphic artist *and* have produced successful book covers for other authors, don't attempt to make your own.

Your cover is the single biggest means to sell your book, so you need the best cover possible. And you aren't the one to do it.

Takeaway: Not every piece of advice applies in every situation or for every writer.

Discover What Type of Writer You Are

Question: I've heard various terms used to describe writers, what are some common types of writers?

Answer: There are several types of writers. They have different motivations, are at various places in their writing journey, and have different goals. Here are five common scenarios:

1. The Aspiring Writer: I've heard many people refer to themselves as aspiring writers. But they're misusing the label. They say aspiring because at this point in their journey they lack the confidence to say they're a writer, so they qualify it by tacking on aspiring.

If this characterization describes you, I encourage you to take a deep breath, drop aspiring, and instead say, "I am a writer." State it with boldness. It will take practice to say with confidence, but you can do it. You are a writer.

In truth, an aspiring writer is someone who doesn't write; they merely want to write—someday. But they'll never get around to it. Yes, they act like a writer. They read books on writing, go to writing conferences, and hang out with other writers. They talk a good game, but it's just talk.

They want to have written, but they don't want to put in the demanding work to sit down and write. They aspire to write, and it ends there.

Don't be someone who aspires to write. Just write.

2. The Hobbyist Writer: Next, we have people who write for fun, write for therapy, or write for family and friends. They're hobbyists. There's nothing wrong with that.

If hobbyist writer accurately describes you, accept it. As a hobbyist, you may not publish much and certainly won't make much money from your work, but you are writing. And that's what's important. Own that label and celebrate it.

But if you want to realize more from your writing, consider moving beyond being a hobbyist.

3. The Passion Project Writer: Some writers have a book they must write. It's a compulsion, a calling. They work hard to produce the best book they can. Then they indie publish it. Then they spend years promoting and marketing their book.

This book is their passion.

But it may be the only book they ever write. Or if they do write other books, these works may fall short because the passion isn't there. And it shows.

There's nothing wrong with having a passion project or being a one-book author. I know many people who wrote one book, and that's it. That's okay. But if you want more, consider the next two categories of writers.

4. The Artist Writer: I know many writers who view themselves as artists. They create wonderful work and produce it regularly. But they only write when the muse hits or when they have a deadline. If they don't feel like writing, they don't. They're often discovery writers (pantsers). Writing speed and output frequency doesn't matter. They're artists, and producing art is all they care about.

If the phrase starving artist comes to mind, it could fit this category of writer. They may not make much from their art, and it's doubtful they'll earn enough to support themselves. That's why the artist writer needs another source of income. This supplemental money could be a day job or a side hustle. It may be a spouse, an inheritance, or a generous patron.

If this is your situation, that's okay. Accept it for who you are, what you want to be, and what works for you.

5. The Career Author: The fifth category is a career author. Although their words may flow from many different motivations, they have one trait in common: writing is their job, and they strive to make money from it, either full-time or part-time.

They haven't sold out. They're being intentional. They value the craft and may even view it as art. They also write with passion. But, in addition to art and passion, they write with purpose. They want to share their words with others and earn money as they do. They have an entrepreneurial mindset. They're an authorpreneur.

My Journey: At various times in my writing journey I have stopped at four of these five writing destinations. Some of my stops have been brief, and others longer, but where I am now—and where I want to remain—is as a career author.

Right now, I make some of my income as a book author, and my goal is to one day earn all my income through books. But money is not my motivator; it's the outcome. My desire is to share my words with others. As I often say, my goal is to "change the world one word at a time." And making money from doing so is a sweet result.

Discover what type of writer you are and embrace it. Don't let anyone tell you your path is wrong or inconsequential. You are a writer. Now own it.

Takeaway: Discovering what type of writer you are will help you find contentment.

MY STORY

I remember it well.

Alone, I sit in my home office. I should be working. I'm not. I'm distracted. In my windowless basement room, I swing the door shut and dim the lights. I know what I must do, but I don't want to.

I've been writing and publishing for years, but I've never owned this reality. Now I must. It's a seminal moment, of that I'm quite sure. If I don't do it today, it might never happen. My gut rumbles. I inhale deeply and close my eyes, as if eyelids will afford me protection from what I'm about to do.

Pulse racing, my lips move, but no sound comes out. On my third attempt, an audible rasp oozes forth, a murmur I can barely hear. Almost indiscernible, I just mumbled, "I am a writer."

I try again. Eventually my volume rises to a normal speaking level, but my words lack confidence. A few months later I try this in front of another person. It emerges as a most pitiful attempt. It takes a couple years before I can confidently tell someone that I'm a writer.

That was a long time ago. Now saying "I am a writer" flows forth without effort and no self-doubt—because it's true.

At writing conferences, I occasionally teach a workshop for newer writers. I often lead my class in saying this phrase out loud: "I am a writer." Their first effort is cautious, timid. But by their third attempt, they grin with confidence. We need to first call ourselves writers if others are to believe it.

I am a writer and so are you.

I sold the first article I ever wrote in 1982 and never stopped. I formed a magazine publishing company in 2001, where I function as publisher and editor-in-chief. In 2008 I began blogging, long before blogging—and later, content marketing—became a thing. And in 2015 I became a successful commercial freelance writer. And I even ghost wrote a couple of books.

Over my career, I've written thousands of blog posts, hundreds of articles, and scores of books, with a hundred ideas in queue, for both nonfiction and fiction.

And like most authors who publish a book about writing, I suffer from imposter syndrome. I suspect this perspective stems from the fact that I'm a self-taught writer. I don't have an MFA degree, and I didn't even study writing in college.

I learned by doing. And that might be the best way to learn.

The benefit of being a self-taught writer is that I studied what I needed to know when I needed to know it. I also followed blogs, read books, and listened to podcasts—many podcasts—about writing and publishing. I went to conferences and attended critique groups. I got feedback on my writing every chance I could get.

But mostly I wrote. I wrote a lot.

Over the years I've learned and grown as a writer. I've received recognition and awards. And I often hear compliments about the way I weave words together. There are many aspects of writing I've learned to do well, other areas where I strive to improve, and one item persists as my Achilles' heel: grammar.

You see, I switched schools between fourth and fifth grade. My old school had not yet even hinted at grammar, while my new school had already covered it thoroughly. I was far behind in grammar when I transferred. And I never caught up.

In college I took only one writing class, a freshman-level requirement. When I took the placement test to gauge my writing ability, I failed the grammar portion in grand fashion. They advised me to take remedial English first. But since they didn't require it, I took the standard freshman writing class they didn't feel I was ready for. Through hard work and a determination that astounded my instructor, I persevered and earned a 4.0. It was my first and last college writing class. After my bachelor's degree, I later went on for a master's and then two PhD's. Along the way I did a lot of writing.

Even though it took me a while to call myself a writer, I've been writing most of my life. In high school I learned I had a knack for it, and it's been part of most every job I've had. Although I've had some great jobs, my work as a full-time writer is the most rewarding thing I've ever done.

Using words to educate and entertain others is an art form that I cherish. Being an author and writing every day is a job so wonderful that it doesn't even feel like work. I get to influence and encourage others with my words. How amazing is that?

I don't plan on ever retiring. I like writing too much to stop. My prayer is that I will be able to write—and write well—until the day I die, which I hope is a long way off.

Until then, I will persist in my goal to change the world one word at a time.

Takeaway: Writing is an amazing, wonderful, and fulfilling adventure. Having a successful career as a writer takes time, effort, and persistence. But it can happen. Just don't rush it.

About Peter Lyle DeHaan

Peter Lyle DeHaan, PhD, is a writer, entrepreneur, and businessman who has managed, owned, and started multiple businesses over his life. A common theme at every turn has been writing, which morphed into his present—and final—career as a fulltime writer.

He shares his lifetime of writing experience, business knowledge, and personal insights through his books, articles, and blogs to encourage, inspire, and occasionally entertain.

His mission is to change the world one word at a time.

Learn more at PeterLyleDeHaan.com.

BOOKS BY PETER DEHAAN

General Market Books as Peter Lyle DeHaan
(PeterLyleDeHaan.com)

Sticky Series:
Sticky Customer Service
Sticky Sales and Marketing

Call Center Success Series:
Healthcare Call Center Essentials
How to Start a Telephone Answering Service

Christian Market Books as Peter DeHaan (PeterDeHaan.com)

Dear Theophilus Bible Study Series:
That You May Know *(the gospel of Luke)*
Tongues of Fire *(the book of Acts)*
For Unto Us *(the prophet Isaiah)*
Return to Me *(the Minor Prophets)*
I Hope in Him *(the book of Job)*
Living Water *(the gospel of John)*
Love Is Patient *(Paul's letters to the Corinthians)*

A New Heaven and a New Earth *(John's Revelation)*
Love One Another *(John's letters)*
Run with Perseverance *(the book of Hebrews)*

Holiday Celebration Bible Study Series:
The Advent of Jesus
The Passion of Jesus
The Victory of Jesus

Bible Character Sketches Series:
Women of the Bible
The Friends and Foes of Jesus
Old Testament Sinners and Saints

Visiting Churches Series:
Shopping for Church
Visiting Online Church
52 Churches
The 52 Churches Workbook
More Than 52 Churches
The More Than 52 Churches Workbook

Other Books:
Jesus's Broken Church
Martin Luther's 95 Theses
Bridging the Sacred-Secular Divide
Beyond Psalm 150
How Big Is Your Tent?